Justice Denied

Crimes in Ireland

Jimmy Guerin

BLACKWATER PRESS

Editor
Sinéad Lawton

Design & Layout
Paula Byrne

Cover Design
Melanie Gradtke

ISBN
1-84131-668-7

© 2004 Jimmy Guerin

Produced in Ireland by
Blackwater Press
c/o Folens Publishers
Hibernian Industrial Estate
Tallaght
Dublin 24

Contents

Acknowledgements

Writing this book has brought me in contact with many people who willingly gave of their time and knowledge, for this I am grateful.

There were a number of Gardaí, both serving and retired, who recalled their experiences and helped as I tried to research the various investigations that were conducted into the crimes that make up this book. While all willingly helped with enthusiasm, they are reluctant to be named as they feel that the authorities will not welcome certain aspects of this book.

As I researched the stories which are covered in this book I came in contact with many people who gave freely of their time and to thank them all would be an onerous task, to name a few would be unfair, so to all who spoke to me, a sincere thanks.

There is one man, however, who was particularly brave and helpful – Jimmy Livingstone. Even though it was difficult, on many occasions Jimmy welcomed me into his home and recalled the stories and events surrounding the tragic killing of his wife Grace. To Jimmy, I say a special thank you.

To the staff at various libraries who on many occasions turned a blind eye to my using a mobile phone, and who often just minutes before closing time would recover one more paper cutting or one more document which was necessary in researching this book.

I would like to thank Sherrie King Gillcrist for kindly reading some of this work as I went along, and making many suggestions that were extremely helpful.

There are others who deserve special mention.

First and most importantly, my wife Louann, who for the last twenty years has been most supportive in everything I have done. Without her support and friendship none of this would have been possible.

Finally I would like to thank John O'Connor and all at Blackwater Press. In particular, the constructive criticism and the valued help given to me by my editor Sinéad Lawton are deeply appreciated. If it were not for her expertise, enthusiasm, and her constant emails and phone calls, this project may never have been completed.

Introduction

Since the beginning of time, our belief system has been based on the theory that the punishment should fit the crime, yet what you are about to read will force you to doubt this belief. It will also force you to re-evaluate all you know about your country, your peacekeepers, and most frighteningly, the people who share the streets and public thoroughfares with you.

These are not fictional stories. They are real life dramas, tales of mayhem and murder played out on the friendly streets of modern day Ireland. Each one remains an unfinished canvas where closure may never be possible for the surviving friends and families.

On the 7 December, 1992, Grace Livingstone, a 56-year-old housewife, was brutally beaten, bound and murdered in her home in Malahide. Her violent death shocked the country, and the people who lived in this small seaside resort in north Co. Dublin were in constant fear, believing that her attacker could, at any moment, strike again. Grace's husband, Jimmy, soon became the prime suspect in her murder. In an investigation that still remains unsolved, Jimmy Livingstone, a senior Revenue official, was accused of shooting his wife, and of then trying to evade justice by giving misleading information to the investigating Gardaí. Jimmy, in turn, claims that someone tried to frame him, and that he is the victim of Garda incompetence, suffering as a result of 'lies, leaks and layabouts'. Jimmy Livingstone and his children are now suing the state over the behaviour of the Gardaí during the course of the investigation into his wife's death.

In 1986, a young boy, Philip Cairns went missing as he headed back to school in the safe suburb of Rathfarnham in Dublin. There have been no positive sightings of him since. This book questions whether various missing persons are really missing, or whether they are in fact the victims of the more serious crime of murder. At the time of Philip's disappearance, there were many rumours, including those of a cult or paedophile ring being responsible for his abduction.

On the 12 October, 1971, Una Lynskey was returning from work to her home in Ratoath, Co. Meath when she suddenly went missing. Within hours, locals were combing the area in an attempt to find her. Soon, the Garda investigation focused on three local youths who were subsequently taken to Trim Garda station where they were questioned for a period of over forty hours. During this period of detention, the young men claim they were beaten and forced to sign confessions admitting to a part in a crime they did not commit. Una's body was later discovered in the Dublin Mountains.

The horror did not end there for this small community. Shortly after Una's remains were found, members of Una's family abducted one of the youths allegedly responsible, and killed him. As he lay dead on the roadside, the Lynskey men then castrated him.

The two surviving youths were later convicted of Una's manslaughter, although one of these decisions was overturned on appeal. Gardaí who were involved in this investigation still maintain that they got the right men, and strongly deny that the men were assaulted or forced to sign confessions while they were in custody.

This is a tragic case, a double tragedy, where the lives of two young people were lost and many of those left behind have still not recovered from these traumatic events.

Richard (Richie) Barron, a cattle dealer and small farmer, was walking home after an eventful night out in his hometown of Raphoe, Co. Donegal, when some unknown person or persons killed him. His death was originally treated as a hit-and-run accident. However, when it was learned that Gardaí had failed to take basic steps at the scene of his death, rumours began circulating in Raphoe that they were covering something up. It was suggested that some Gardaí may have been involved in the crime, but two local men were subsequently arrested and questioned over Richie's death. Their treatment while in Garda custody and that of others arrested was the subject of an internal Garda investigation which uncovered serious corruption at the highest levels of the Gardaí in the Donegal division. There have been allegations of false confessions, forged signatures, extortion and Gardaí beating suspects while in custody. Another garda involved in the investigation refuses to account for his movements and whereabouts at the time Richie was murdered. The investigation resulted in the establishment of a tribunal of inquiry, which has confirmed that the levels of corruption which exist in our police force are unmatched in most civilised countries. Today various parties, including the McBreartys, are suing the Gardaí over their behaviour during this investigation while the killer of Richie Barron remains at large.

On 26 June, 1996, Veronica Guerin, a 36-year-old mother and one of Ireland's leading investigative journalists, was brutally murdered by a pillion passenger on a motorbike, driven by drug dealer and gang member Brian Meehan. Veronica's death resulted in an unprecedented police investigation and the smashing of Ireland's largest criminal gang. The dedicated team investigating her death, headed up by one of the most respected and experienced Garda in the state, Assistant Commissioner Tony Hickey, worked tirelessly to bring the gang responsible for Veronica's murder to justice.

Veronica's death resulted in the establishment of the witness protection programme, which saw the man who loaded the gun and possibly fired the shots which killed her being set up overseas in a new life at the expense of the taxpayer. It also saw the establishment of the Criminal Assets Bureau, which has set about seizing the assets of well known criminals, and which in the past year has targeted politicians and government officials who have been found guilty of corruption.

This book looks at trial transcripts, confessions and statements, some of which have not been in the public domain before now. It exposes the level of corruption among those who are charged with investigating crime in this country, which has resulted in many people losing all faith in our system of justice. All sides of each case are presented here, comments from officers from the investigations alongside those of the loved ones left behind. Some of these cases could yet prove to be a major embarrassment to both the Gardaí and the state.

What is extraordinary about these crimes is that they happened to ordinary people. People like you and me going about their daily business in life, never once suspecting that they were living their final day on this earth. Each story will be familiar to you. The victims of these crimes deserve justice, yet it appears that they have been denied this, but who is to blame? I have put the facts and the research before you. This time you be the judge.

Jimmy Guerin
November 2004

For Louann

1

Grace Livingstone

At the age of 56, Grace Livingstone appeared to be a woman who had it all. She had been married for over 25 years and was a devoted mother. Neighbours describe her as a quietly spoken woman, who had a small but close circle of friends. She had a love of flowers and plants, and was well known locally through her membership of the horticultural society and the Portmarnock flower arrangers. Grace also helped at her local church and assisted at 9 am mass each morning. Afterwards she would take her dog for a long walk on Portmarnock Strand or enjoy the extensive grounds of Malahide Castle, which was close to her home.

Grace had a comfortable house that she had made into a lovely home. She lived in The Moorings, an affluent area of Malahide, a small seaside town in North County Dublin, with her husband, Jimmy. Grace's husband held one of the most senior posts in the Revenue Commissioners and they wanted for nothing. With good neighbours and two grown-up children, life was good for the Livingstone family.

A friend of Grace's for more than twenty years described her as an 'old-fashioned upper-class lady, the type you would expect to see married to a vicar. She was an attractive woman and universally liked. She was also an extremely friendly woman. I could not imagine any person disliking Grace.'

Grace and Jimmy Livingstone were married on 1 October, 1968. Friends describe them as total opposites, which was evident from the different interests they had. However, Jimmy describes

Grace as the 'cornerstone of my existence'. Sometimes, when he went shooting, Grace would accompany him and collect flowers. She also often accompanied him when he went fishing, and was even known to try her hand at angling. Jimmy smiles as he recalls, 'Grace's angling skills would create little danger to the stock of fish in the country.' But it was not her skill that was important, it was the fact that she was there with him. They were, according to Jimmy, 'a close family unit that enjoyed the time they spent together'.

On the morning of 7 December, 1992, Grace went about her day as normal. She attended morning mass and followed this with a walk in the grounds of Malahide Castle. Her thoughts were most likely with her daughter, Tara, who lived in France and was expecting her first child. This would be Grace's first grandchild, and she was extremely excited about the forthcoming event. Grace had just sent Tara a Christmas cake and a substantial gift of money to buy herself things she might need following the birth.

Later that afternoon, Grace went out for a short walk, and as she returned home to make the evening meal, she spoke with neighbours. According to witness statements, Grace Livingstone was last seen alive at around 4.30 pm on the day of her murder.

***

Some time between 4.30 pm and 5.50 pm on the afternoon of 7 December, Grace was violently attacked and killed in the very home she loved. Forensic evidence indicates that her attacker hit her on the back of the head and she then fell forward, possibly hitting her face on the floor or furniture. Her attacker then bound her legs and arms with tape, covered her mouth and carried her upstairs to her own bedroom where he or she placed her face down on the bed.

Evidence indicates that the attacker then walked to the wardrobe where Jimmy Livingstone kept his firearms, and removed a shotgun and ammunition. This was the only wardrobe that was disturbed. He or she then returned to Grace, who was bound and lay helpless on the bed, took a pillow and placed it over her head. The attacker then placed the gun under the pillow and lay it almost horizontal to her spine, pulled the trigger and shot her in the head, killing her instantly. By holding the gun in such a position, it would have saved the killer from kickback and also reduced the possibility of trace evidence. It was obvious the killer knew about guns.

The killer then walked down the stairs, shotgun in hand, opened the hall door and left. As soon as he or she walked out of the house, the killer slid the shotgun under a hedge just below the window at the front of the house.

***

Jimmy Livingstone left his office shortly before 5 pm on the evening that Grace was murdered. He was anxious to get home early. That evening both he and Grace were due to drive to Monaghan to attend an anniversary mass for Jimmy's brother, who had died in 1987. As Jimmy Livingstone left work and headed for home, he was delayed in unusually heavy traffic.

'I didn't get a good run because traffic was lousy', he recalls. 'I had to drop Art O'Connor, a fellow civil servant, home. He lives close by and I left him off about 5.50 pm, and arrived to my own home at 5.55.'

In an interview with RTÉ radio some months following Grace's murder, Jimmy recalled his arrival home: 'On that particular day, 7 December, 1992, I arrived home and I turned my car outside the door, which is not what I normally did. I parked it in front of the driveway. I came down the driveway. The first thing I noticed was that the light wasn't on in the porch ... Another thing I noticed was that the curtains in the converted garage were drawn. Now, that was not normal. Grace kept flower plants on the windowsill of the converted garage and the curtains were never drawn ... I came into the house and the normal thing would be that the dog would greet me, which he didn't. The other thing was, I did not get the smell of cooking and where I could see into the kitchen, the table wasn't set ...

'I came into the kitchen and there was dirt on the floor where it had been swept and not put away and the brush was there; I think the brush was there. Grace wasn't there, of course. I looked in the dining room, the sitting room and the playroom ... I looked down the back. I didn't see her. I didn't hear the dog and I slightly wondered.

'I went upstairs thinking that possibly she had taken ill or something and had gone up and lain down. I got to the top of the stairs and I noticed, outside my son's bedroom, a canvas case which holds a .22 rifle lying against the door, and that was unusual, but there could be an explanation for that. He could have left it lying on a suit and the mother may have told him to get that oily gun out of his wardrobe. That was a possible explanation.

'I went to the bedroom and I did not put on the light in the bedroom. I went into the bedroom from the light of the landing and the reason for this was that if she had gone up and lay down because she was ill, or something had happened, she wouldn't want the light flashing on her.

'I went into the room and I did notice, as my eyes geared to the reduced light in the room, I noticed some pillows or what I subsequently thought were pillows at the far end of the bed and that was just a wee bit extraordinary, but maybe she had pushed the pillows to one side. Then as my eyes geared to the light I saw her form lying on the bed. I went up the side of the bed and put my hand out to touch her forehead. I felt it wet. My first thought was, "Lord, she is after vomiting on the bed." I then went to put the light on. When I put the light on I discovered it wasn't vomit. It was blood and her whole insides.

'I looked at her, the mess, and I froze. There was a hole in her head. I jumped around a little, I danced, I panicked and I certainly wasn't thinking straight. I thought, "Do I untie her? Do I turn her over? What do I do?"'

Soon Jimmy gathered his thoughts and ran to the house of a neighbour, who is a nurse.

'I called to the home of Mrs Watchorn, a nurse, but she wasn't home. So then I called to the home of another neighbour, Margaret Murphy, who is a retired nurse. A young child answered the door and I told him, "Get your mammy quick, it's very urgent, there's been an accident."'

Jimmy ran back to his house and called for an ambulance. The call was recorded at 5.58 pm.

'My name is Jimmy Livingstone of 37 The Moorings, Malahide. There's been a terrible accident. I have an injured woman. It's some form of assault. I need an ambulance.'

He was asked if the woman had collapsed outside his home and he replied, 'No, I came in from work and found her lying on the bed with her hands tied behind her back. She needs an ambulance.'

He then called the Gardaí who arrived at his home within minutes. While he was awaiting the arrival of the ambulance and the Gardaí, Jimmy Livingstone went back to his bedroom and assisted Margaret Murphy, who was tending to Grace.

Mrs Murphy was unable to determine if there was a pulse because Grace was bound so tightly. Jimmy Livingstone removed a small pair of scissors that he always carried from his pocket and cut the tape to allow Mrs Murphy to remove it. He himself never touched the tape. The fact that he did not assist in removing the tape led the Gardaí to speculate that even at this early stage, Jimmy Livingstone was being careful not do anything which would implicate him in Grace's murder.

***

Thus began an unimaginable horror in Jimmy Livingstone's life. Within hours he believed that the Gardaí considered him a suspect, and it soon transpired that he was right. Jimmy not only faced the bleak loss brought by this most vicious and savage murder, but now he faced a double torment, his wife was dead and he was being accused of this most horrific crime.

When Detective Sergeant Cathal Cryan, an experienced investigator, arrived at the scene, he too noticed things that seemed out of kilter, small things that only an experienced eye would see. He observed that there was no sign of forced entry, no sign of a struggle. When he went upstairs, he noticed the gun and case on the landing. When he entered the room where Grace had been murdered, he noticed that there was a bloodstain on the light switch. He found this strange, and at first it led him to believe that the perpetrator had had blood on his hands when he brought Grace to the room to kill her. Jimmy Livingstone later said that he switched the lights on after he felt Grace's forehead and it was he who had put the blood on the light switch.

Cathal Cryan was not the most senior officer by rank in attendance, but he was undoubtedly the most experienced, having investigated hundreds of serious crimes. He introduced himself to Jimmy Livingstone and then began to question him. One of the first things that Cryan tried to establish was if any of the guns were missing. Jimmy replied that he did not know, explaining that he had not yet checked.

Cryan felt uneasy, he was aware that this was a traumatic time for Jimmy Livingstone, but still felt that he was being over cautious for someone who had just found his wife murdered. Cryan was also surprised to note that the killer had known exactly where to locate the weapons. He also found it strange that such a gun enthusiast as Jimmy Livingstone, who would be aware of the guidelines about keeping weapons at home, had stored ammunition in the same place as the guns.

Cryan spoke to a number of his colleagues at the scene. They agreed that something was not right. Little things that they found unusual, like the lack of forced entry, the gun on the landing, no sign of a struggle and the fact that the dog was out the back, led some of them to suspect that Grace's husband Jimmy could have been involved in this awful crime.

The ambulance men and the doctor arrived and, after they had tended to Grace, the Gardaí gave permission for the body to be removed from the house.

After Grace's body had been removed from her home, Jimmy Livingstone and Cathal Cryan went to the living room, where other Gardaí were discussing the crime, what had been observed and various theories as to what might have occurred. Then a shotgun was found outside the front window of the house, under the hedge beside the front door. Gardaí immediately suspected they had recovered the murder weapon, and Jimmy Livingstone identified the gun as his.

Jimmy explained it some months later as follows: 'I was talking to the police; they were saying there was no sign of a struggle. We were standing in the front room and [Detective Inspector] Frank Gunne asked me, "Is that your gun?" I looked out the window and said, "Yes". Again the police are making an issue of that. They're saying it was dark and how could I recognise my gun? Well I recognised my gun because it had scratch marks on it that gave it a piebald colouring. I knew it was mine even if it was dark.'

Cathal Cryan, however, sees it differently: 'We were in the front room and looking out the window. There was a garda standing, say, two or three yards from the gun, shining his torch on it. The lights were on in the room. I was standing beside Jimmy Livingstone when he identified the gun. I could not see it clearly. I do not know how he was able to recognise the gun as his. He had told us some minutes earlier that he did not know if one of his guns was missing. He only had a few guns, not an arsenal, so I would have expected him to have checked if one was missing before he made a positive identification.'

One hour after making the call to the Gardaí to report his wife's murder, Jimmy Livingstone accompanied two guards, Detective Garda Palmer and Detective Sergeant Cathal Cryan, to Malahide Garda station. What was obvious from that evening was that the two men central to the investigation, Cryan and Livingstone, mistrusted each other from the start. Livingstone claims that he was not happy with the line of questioning, and Cryan felt he was not being told the whole story. Jimmy Livingstone felt that Cryan's attitude in the house had been arrogant and believes that he was shown no sympathy for the loss he had suffered. Cryan, on the other hand, believes that Livingstone was cold in the house, and was not behaving in a manner consistent with a man who had just discovered his wife brutally murdered.

Jimmy Livingstone entered Malahide Garda station at about 7 pm and spent the next eight hours being questioned about his movements during that day. He did not mind going through this procedure. In fact it was Jimmy himself who had offered to give information to the Gardaí saying, 'I was anxious to assist and help find Grace's killer.' Jimmy agreed to accompany the detectives to the station, and according to Gardaí, was aware that he could leave at any time.

Jimmy Livingstone had attended his office early on the morning his wife was murdered. The office is located in the centre of Dublin, about ten miles from Jimmy's home, a journey that could take up to an hour, depending on traffic. He worked through till lunchtime, and then went for a swim with colleagues, which was a weekly event. On his way back to the office, Jimmy went to a nearby ATM machine and withdrew money; he still has the transaction slip, which proves he was there at the time he stated.

Jimmy is able to account for his movements all day, most significantly the fact that he had been in the company of another civil servant up until five minutes before he discovered Grace's body.

He recalls, 'On that day I had a profile in the office with regard to a particular job that was going on, and I was in touch with my staff for the whole day at approximately half-hourly intervals and this has all been authenticated by my staff for the entire day, that I was there, and this has been given to the guards. There has been no unaccounted period in my day on the 7 December and the guards are quite aware of that. Nor have they challenged me or been able to challenge me in regard to my movements on that day.'

Jimmy later complained to his solicitor about the way he had been treated while at the station on the night of his wife's murder. One of the things he mentioned to his solicitor was that he had told Detective Sergeant Cryan that he was turning the interview into a very tedious process. He also claimed that Cryan and Palmer were not recording the answers accurately in the words in which they were being given. During the interview, Detective Sergeant Cryan absented himself on two occasions, once for 20 minutes and another time for 40 minutes. Jimmy Livingstone raised this issue and also Cryan's general behaviour with him, and suggested that the interview should proceed at a more constant pace. Jimmy Livingstone claims the answer he received from Cryan was less than reassuring.

Jimmy was unaware that on one of the occasions that Cryan left, he called to the home of Art O'Connor, the man to whom Jimmy had given a lift home on the day Grace was killed. Cryan was checking up on the detail of times that were being given to him. It was another sign that the relationship between Jimmy Livingstone and Cathal Cryan had got of to a bad start and it became more and more confrontational.

Jimmy's experience in the station that night was not what one would expect for a man who was there of his own free will, and who was trying to assist Gardaí in their efforts to catch the man who had just murdered his wife some hours earlier. During the time he was in the station, a period of over seven hours, Jimmy claims he was offered no refreshments, not shown where the bathroom was and not told that his son was there until some hours after his arrival. The investigation could not have got off on a worse footing.

At 3 am on 8 December, Jimmy Livingstone had his statement read over to him. He was asked to sign it, but he declined. Jimmy now accepts that his refusal to sign his statement really annoyed the interviewing detectives, but claims that his answers had not been accurately recorded.

***

Interviews and investigations were not new to Jimmy Livingstone as he was a senior Revenue official. At the time of Grace's murder, he headed up the tax evasion branch. Day after day, Jimmy was involved in interviews, at times with hostile people who did not want to reveal any details of their affairs. He had spent most of his adult life in the FCÁ (the army section of the Reserve Defence Force) and was also a former member of the military police. For most of his working life, Jimmy Livingstone had moved in worlds where keen focus is the tool which brings results.

The late Jim Mitchell acknowledged Jimmy's investigative skills when he was chairman of the public accounts committee that investigated Irish banks and the whole question of fraudulent non-resident accounts. Mitchell said: 'Mr Livingstone's superb investigative skills should be rewarded by the state as they played a major part in exposing the fraud committed by the banks.' Livingstone did, in fact, receive a special payment from the state as a result of Mitchell's remarks.

When Jimmy Livingstone went to Malahide Garda station that night to assist the Gardaí, he went there with faith in a system of which he himself was a part.

'When the Gardaí arrived at my home the night Grace was killed, I had no other thought but to assist them. It was the natural order of things. It was the way to find her killer. At 6.45 pm, less that an hour after I arrived home, I entered Malahide Garda station in the belief that I was assisting in detecting a murderer. In the following eight hours I was to lose faith in the capacity of the detective branch of An Garda Síochána.'

When Jimmy Livingstone left the station on the night that his wife was murdered, he was already suspicious of the competence of the investigation. He believed from the line of questioning that some detectives had already decided that he was responsible for his wife's murder.

On hearing the awful news of Grace's murder, Livingstone's relations made their way to Malahide to be with Jimmy and his son Conor. It had been decided that Jimmy and Conor, who lived at home, would stay with relations on the Swords Road that night.

The following day, Jimmy Livingstone returned to Malahide Garda station as he needed to get access to his home to collect essential items of clothing for himself and his son. When he arrived at the station, he was advised that he could go to the house accompanied to collect items of clothing, but that he could not have his car as the Gardaí had decided to retain it for forensic examination.

Two days later, the keys of his car were returned to him at the relative's house where he and Conor had been staying. He was informed that the Gardaí no longer required his car so he went to collect it at Santry Garda station. When he got the car back, Livingstone claims that various items had been taken from it and the steering lock had been damaged.

The following day, Friday, 11 December, just four days following her murder, the small seaside town of Malahide came to a complete standstill as the funeral mass took place for Grace Livingstone. The mass was celebrated at the local Church of St Sylvester, where the celebrant, former parish priest and family friend Cannon Macartan, told those present how Grace, who was a woman of deep faith, loved to help in the church, and he spoke of her popularity amongst her peers. Fifteen minutes before her funeral mass started, the church was packed tight. There were hundreds of mourners in the church and as many again outside.

It was obvious that people were shocked at the horrible death Grace had suffered. A lot of the mourners were aware that Jimmy Livingstone was a suspect. Detectives mingled with the crowd in the hope that they would pick up some clue, a motive, something that would point them in the direction of Grace's killer.

Shortly before the mass began, Jimmy arrived with his son Conor and his daughter Tara, who had missed the removal the previous night as she had been in Paris when her mother was murdered. After the mass, the funeral made the short journey to Malahide cemetery where Grace was laid to rest.

Jimmy recalls that were it not for the faith that his family, friends and colleagues had in him at that time, he does not know how he would have survived the ordeal. 'Despite the misinformation being leaked by the police, the affection from those close to me, and others, never diminished in any way. I will always be grateful to people for that.'

***

One reason that the murder of Grace Livingstone may never be solved is that the animosity ignited between Jimmy Livingstone and Detective Sergeant Cryan on the night of the crime steadily grew. Details of interviews, which should have remained confidential, were leaked to the media and began appearing in newspaper articles. Jimmy Livingstone was spoken of as a suspect. He was reading about developments in his wife's case in the media before he was being informed by the Gardaí. The Gardaí had shut Jimmy Livingstone out; he was totally frustrated and could not believe how he and his family were being treated.

In an interview some months after her death, Jimmy said that a negative slant was being put on his relationship with Grace. 'It's sickening to think of the slur that has been put on the relationship I had with a very fine person. If this is the Gardaí's form of criminal investigation, it's no surprise to me that the crime rate is what it is. One headline at the weekend said "Gardaí Dismiss Husband's Theories". What they are dismissing are the facts of my alibi. How can they overcome that?'

At the first interview he had with Gardaí, Jimmy Livingstone gave details of a number of Revenue cases he was investigating. He gave this information in the belief that certain individuals involved may have wanted to frighten or harm him. He believes that these leads were never properly investigated.

Shortly after Grace's killing, Jimmy was asked in an interview if the killer could have been a person whose tax affairs he had exposed. He replied, 'It is a possibility. If that was so it would be very difficult to identify. I have been at our game for a very long time and I am sure that, in the course of work, I have caused distress to people I have never even noticed. That is the way it is.'

When asked if he was ever threatened he replied, 'I am not aware of any threat ever having been made to me. Maybe I am the type of person who wouldn't be looking for a threat or wouldn't accept a threat. I think you could be over-romantic about that. I am not aware of anybody having threatened me. I know I have dealt with serious tax evaders and I know some of them would have the capacity to do this [murder Grace], but none of them ever threatened me; none of them ever made a direct approach. But, as to whether they did it or not, I don't know.'

There was one suspect, however, that Jimmy Livingstone had in mind as he was giving details to the Gardaí and also in newspaper interviews some months following Grace's death. This was Thomas 'Slab' Murphy, a well-known Republican with business interests on both sides of the border, described by Livingstone as a 'commercial patriot'. Livingstone had been involved in an investigation into some of Murphy's companies. This had resulted in one of them going into liquidation just days before a meeting with Livingstone and his staff.

Within weeks of the killing, Slab Murphy was mentioned in the papers as one of those named by Jimmy Livingstone. Yet Jimmy Livingstone maintains that no effort was made to follow up those he felt might have wanted to intimidate him, and he took the view that the Gardaí would not follow up his suspicions because of Murphy's fearsome reputation. Murphy's farm was unique as it was located on both sides of the border. He was widely regarded as leader of the Provisional IRA and was undoubtedly one of the most feared men on the island. Members of security forces on both sides of the border were always worried when they would have to visit the Murphy farm, and this always necessitated a huge security operation to guarantee their safety.

Such reluctance to follow up potential leads is dismissed as rubbish by the leading investigator on the case, Detective Sergeant Cryan. He had no interest in Murphy's reputation or any other issues that special branch or other Gardaí divisions may have had with Slab Murphy. He was investigating the murder of Grace Livingstone and he says this was his primary concern.

Cathal Cryan and his colleagues were totally satisfied that Slab Murphy, notorious IRA man, was not involved in the murder of Grace Livingstone because they did not accept that Murphy would carry out such a crime just because his company's tax affairs were being investigated. Furthermore, on the day of the funeral, the IRA had issued a statement saying that they 'wished to refute a suggestion that they had in any way been involved in the murder of Grace Livingstone'. The statement was signed P O'Neill, which is the code name that has been used on all statements issued by the IRA since the Troubles began. The Gardaí knew that if the IRA had been involved in this horrific crime, they would not have issued such a statement. However, Jimmy was adamant that this should be investigated and this is why they checked out Slab Murphy after the statement was issued. Cryan decided that he would go and deal with the Murphy aspect of the case himself.

Through contacts he had established over the previous 27 years, Cryan was able to get a mobile number for Slab Murphy. This in itself showed that Cryan had access to a network that even some of the most senior active republicans could not reach.

Cryan recalls, 'I rang up Slab Murphy. In the normal course of events I would have doorstepped him. However, we could not doorstep Slab because you don't know if the door you should call to is in the north or south. Had I doorstepped him, he would have closed down and I would not have received the information I was seeking.'

Cryan says that when he rang Murphy on his mobile, the first thing Murphy wanted to know was where he had got the number. Murphy was not at all pleased at this breach in his personal security. Cryan says, 'I told him that I wished to speak to him about the murder of Grace Livingstone. He understood this as he had been indirectly named in the papers. When we spoke it was not confrontational, and after some discussion he asked where I wanted to meet.'

Murphy told Cryan that he was quite welcome to go to his home, provided that he travelled alone. Cryan said that he never travelled alone and that a colleague would be with him. After some discussion it was agreed that the men would meet at 4 pm at

Hackballscross Garda station in Co. Louth. Murphy had agreed to meet Cryan on two conditions: first that the detective would not wear a wire, and second that no one be advised in advance of their meeting. Slab Murphy was anxious that if it were known he was to attend the police station, the place would be crawling with special branch personnel, who would use the opportunity to photograph him and maybe lift him for questioning in relation to other crimes that were being investigated. Cryan agreed to the conditions as neither compromised his investigation.

On the day they were to meet, Cryan and his colleague were delayed while travelling through Drogheda. As a result, they were less than five minutes late for the meeting. Cryan had intended to arrive some 30 minutes early so he could pay the local Gardaí the courtesy of informing them that Murphy would be attending their station.

'When we arrived at the station we were four minutes late. Murphy had been and gone. To make matters worse, the local sergeant was dancing a jig saying that they had not been informed that Slab Murphy, alleged leader of the IRA, would be attending his station. Murphy left the station at five minutes past four, saying he was going to Dundalk and would not be back.'

Cryan knew it was important that he speak with Murphy and decided to call him again on his mobile phone. Murphy had left his phone at home and Cryan found himself speaking to Slab Murphy's wife Rose, who he describes as an 'absolute charmer'. Cryan apologised that he and his colleague had been delayed in Drogheda, and told her that he was still anxious to speak with her husband. She explained that she had been aware that Murphy was going to the station, and although Slab had told the gardaí at the station that he would not be returning, he would in fact be returning to Hackballcross and they would have their meeting. Cryan was still talking to Rose Murphy when Slab came into the house. She put her husband on the phone to Cryan. 'I expected a lambasting,' says Cryan, 'but while a bit gruff, he was all right. He agreed to come back down to the station.'

Cryan says that he and Murphy had a long discussion in which Murphy described the allegation that he was behind the murder of Grace Livingstone as totally outrageous. Cryan reflects, 'Jimmy Livingstone had led both us and his management to believe that he had had a confrontation with Murphy. According to Murphy this was not the case.'

Murphy told Cryan that he had only ever met Jimmy Livingstone once, at his accountant's office in Dundalk. According to Murphy, Jimmy asked that he be introduced to Slab Murphy that day. Murphy could hardly remember him, and as far as he was concerned, he was just another Revenue inspector up from Dublin. Murphy told Cryan that he was not in least bit concerned about the Revenue because he had liquidated the company in question prior to the meeting with Jimmy.

The Gardaí were not surprised when they eliminated Slab Murphy from their enquiries and had in fact been telling the media that they did not accept that any paramilitary group or individual Republican were involved.

While Jimmy was claiming the leads he was giving the Gardaí were not being followed up, the team of investigators were in fact eliminating all those Jimmy had named.

As well as Slab Murphy, Jimmy had mentioned various other names to the investigators on the first night he was interviewed. These included a bank manager from Munster, whose branch had been investigated by the Revenue after an informer suggested that there had been a sharp rise in deposits at the branch. The investigation had revealed that the bank had opened accounts in false names. However, it is unlikely that the manager would have held a grudge against Jimmy over this affair as the manager's career didn't suffer as a result of the Revenue findings.

Another man named by Jimmy was a businessman based in the mid-west. When he was interviewed by the Gardaí, he recalled what he described as an amicable meeting with Livingstone with an exchange of pleasantries and niceties.

Another man named had never even heard of Jimmy Livingstone and could not understand why he had been mentioned.

One furniture manufacturer based in Meath had had a confrontation with officials from the Revenue when they called to his premises in 1987. This was some five years before the murder of Grace. At the time, staff from Jimmy's office had called the Gardaí in order to gain access. This man was shocked when he was questioned by investigating Gardaí, and although he met members of Jimmy's staff, he claimed that he had never heard of or met Jimmy Livingstone in his life.

Cryan and his investigators were treating these accusations against people with great scepticism. At a meeting between Cryan and Jimmy Livingstone on Saturday, 12 December, 1992, just five days after Grace's murder, Jimmy made clear his mistrust of the Gardaí and seemed prepared to consider anyone as a suspect for his wife's murder. The following extract is taken from the notes of the interview made by Detective Sergeant Cryan at the time.

Cryan: Sit down Mr Livingstone. There are a number of matters related to the suspects nominated for the murder of your wife that we wish to discuss with you. There were a number of investigations involving other people.

Livingstone: Including a good number of Gardaí?

Cryan: No Gardaí, no.

Livingstone: Which makes me wonder about everything.

Cryan: Is there any particular Gardaí I should investigate?

Livingstone: Of course there is.

Cryan: You did nominate a number of people yourself.

Livingstone: I did. I nominated a Garda; I have to live with hard secrets. I don't know if I should say any more about this.

Cryan: In what respect?

Livingstone: There are 11,000 Gardaí in the state. It's an institution, and with institutions, the first thing they protect is the institution.

Cryan: Yeah?

Livingstone: That's a fact. This would happen in the civil service. It would happen in taxes. It happens in the army. It happens with doctors. It happens with solicitors. It's a fact of life.

Cryan: Gardaí in relation to tax evasion?

Livingstone: The basic thing I would like to say, and never forget this, is tax evasion is a criminal offence.

Cryan: Can we get back to the basics of this case. Obviously we are trying to establish a motive for Grace's killing.

Livingstone: It's as simple as this. If I found a garda with a lot of money ...

Cryan: But you're not suggesting, I sincerely hope, that some garda is in some way involved?

Livingstone: I don't know, I don't know.

***

Jimmy Livingstone, through his post in the Revenue Commissioners, had access to any tax records he wanted. A number of Gardaí working on the murder investigation became aware that Jimmy had begun to investigate their affairs. One very senior garda, who ran a small construction business with his son, was investigated, and Jimmy told another garda that he had looked at all the tax affairs of the Gardaí working on the case. Gardaí also recovered a notebook belonging to Jimmy Livingstone, which had the tax numbers of all the Gardaí involved in this case noted in it.

On one occasion, Jimmy called to Malahide Garda station and went into the public office. He had with him the tax file belonging to Detective Sergeant Cathal Cryan. Cryan recalls, 'One day he arrived at the station with my private tax records, shouting out of him how much overtime I was earning.' Cryan regrets he was not there as he claims he would have taken the files from him and thrown him out of the station.

Cryan believes that because of who Jimmy is, he was treated differently from the beginning. This, Cryan believes, was a serious mistake on the part of the Gardaí. He remembers that on the third day of the investigation they became aware that some of the guns Jimmy had in his house were illegally owned, including a .45 revolver. When Cryan went to a conference that was being held by officers involved in the hunt for Grace's killer, he commented that if Livingstone lived in Darndale and the circumstances were all the same, he would have already been arrested.

'If I went into a house in Darndale, and I found the lady of the house deceased in her bedroom, and don't forget she was carried to the room she was in – the murderer actually brought her to her own bed. Why not another room? ... We had the victim dead in her own bed, in a room where her husband stores his guns, and she is shot with her husband's gun. Then the killer, whoever he is, decides to remove the gun from the scene, brings it downstairs and dumps it at the front door. Then on searching the house we find a number of illegal guns, including a revolver and holster ... Now if that had occurred in Darndale, the man of the house would have been arrested straight away because of the guns.'

It would appear that Livingstone also felt he was different from the people of Darndale. In an interview some months after Grace's murder he said, 'They knew they weren't dealing with the guilty or innocent from Darndale, they were dealing with Jimmy Livingstone and I know the law.'

Speaking of the Gardaí and the way they dealt with him, he also said: 'I know their techniques, they've tried to break me, but their boorishness might work, as I said, with the guilty or even the innocent of Darndale, but it won't work with Jimmy Livingstone.'

***

On 29 December, 1992, just three weeks after Grace was murdered, Jimmy Livingstone had arranged to attend Malahide Garda station for further interviews. He stayed from 10 am to 7 pm. He left the station when he received a telephone call from his daughter Tara.

According to Jimmy Livingstone it had been arranged that a Ban Garda would go to his house at 3 pm that day to interview Tara, who was heavily pregnant. Cathal Cryan says, however, that it had not been prearranged that a Ban Garda would take Tara's statement: 'In fact it was only decided after consultation with Detective Superintendent Mick Maguire that I go to the house. We knew from [Livingstone's] initial statements that there had been difficulties between Tara and her father, and felt it was important to speak with her while he was not present at the house. It was at this stage that I phoned her.'

While Livingstone was at the station he received a call from his home. It was his daughter Tara in what he describes as a very distressed state. Tara claims that she had received a call from Cryan, who asked her why she had failed to attend Malahide station earlier that day as agreed. Tara alleges that she told Cryan that this was not correct, as it had been arranged that a garda would call and see her at home at 3 pm that afternoon. Cryan told her that the interview would have to be brought forward, and he called to her house within a few minutes of making the call.

Tara claims that Cryan told her that her father had been partying all over Christmas, even though his wife had just been murdered. She also claims that Cryan asked if her father and mother had lovers, if she had ever been beaten by her father, and if she was aware that her father was an alcoholic. Tara became extremely upset and requested that Cryan leave. She claims that at first he refused to go, she got up, opened the door and ordered him out of the house. He only left the house, however, when Jimmy Livingstone arrived with the Inspector who he had been assisting at Malahide, and it was, according to Cryan, the Inspector who ordered him from the house.

Cryan recalls going to the Livingstone home and interviewing Tara, but denies that he was abusive towards her. He stresses that he would have no reason whatsoever to be offensive. 'Under no circumstances would I say anything to a daughter about her late mother. The reason that I mentioned that her father had been partying was because we had tried on a number of occasions to interview him over the Christmas period, and because of commitments he had, he had been unavailable. I would not have been confrontational with this witness.'

Tara immediately phoned her father at the station as she was extremely upset. Jimmy Livingstone was driven to his home by a senior garda. Detective Cryan was asked to leave the house and did. Livingstone did not return to the station that day, instead he stayed at home and comforted his daughter.

***

Less than a month later, Detective Sergeant Cryan and Jimmy Livingstone were to confront each other again. This time they met in a room in the Revenue building where Jimmy worked. According to Jimmy this room was made available to Cryan so that he could interview Jimmy's colleagues about his movements on the day of the murder, and answer questions about him as their boss. However, the fact is that the room had been made available to the investigating Gardaí so that they could review the files Jimmy had been working on at the time of Grace's death. They wanted to see if there was any evidence to substantiate Jimmy's fears that someone being investigated might have had a motive or wanted to intimidate him.

According to Jimmy, Cryan interviewed him in this office in the Revenue building in January 1993. 'He [Cryan] stated that he reckoned that I had plenty of time to go to Malahide during the day Grace was killed, and gave the impression that he had come to this conclusion from his interviews with my staff. He referred to my long absence at lunchtime on the day.'

Jimmy maintains that such a deduction was absolutely illogical. 'I was devastated by his remarks, which were the most direct accusations that he had made to date.' He told Cryan about his visit to the ATM machine and says, 'He told me that I had planned it all very well, but that he would prove his case and he would see me suffer. When I withdrew from the office I was shattered.'

This account is in total opposition with Cryan's account. Cryan had been accompanied by another officer that day. 'We had told Jimmy's superior that we wished to interview Jimmy concerning some of the files. At 12.30 pm, he requested Livingstone to report to the room we were in after lunch. I made no such remarks about his being absent from the office during lunch [on the day of the murder], as I never ever suspected that Grace was killed early in the day. We never attended the offices to check out his movements, as we were satisfied with the details of his movements on the day Grace was murdered.

'There was one moment when he seemed a bit shaken and that was when we requested that he give us a sample of his voice so that we could check it against a caller who had left messages about the case. He was reluctant, but did agree to provide us with the sample. I would accept that I may have put difficult questions to him, but this would have been done when he was arrested over the illegal firearms and in custody in Swords station.'

Cryan suspected that Jimmy had been making anonymous calls to the Gardai, where the caller said he had knowledge of who killed Grace Livingstone and implied that the murder was related to Jimmy's work. Cryan believed that Jimmy was the man on the phone and even went to the UK after he retired to have tests carried out on the recordings to establish if the voice was in fact that of Jimmy Livingstone. The tests, however, proved negative.

The confrontation that day had a telling effect on Jimmy Livingstone, who told another senior Revenue colleague that he was now concerned that the investigating Gardaí would try to frame him. He admits that he became extremely worried and depressed, and was concerned about what might happen. Unknown to Jimmy, his colleague went to the Chairman of the Revenue Commissioners and told him of Jimmy's concerns. According to Jimmy, the Chairman contacted him, and at a meeting between the two men, assured him of the full support of all of his colleagues. Jimmy believes that he enjoyed this support up to his retirement from the Revenue in 2001. The person who went to the Chairman had reason to believe Jimmy's concerns. He had been with Jimmy Livingstone at crucial times on the day Grace was murdered, and had provided this information to the police. He was visited on four separate occasions about the times he gave in his statement and felt he was being unduly pressurised. At one stage, this official considered legal action against the Gardaí over what he saw as harassment.

Cryan recalls the many conversations that he had with Jimmy Livingstone's staff and remembers that there was a lot of resentment towards Jimmy. 'Let me put it this way, I did not leave that day thinking that this person was being supported by his staff and felt that none of them were surprised that I wished to question them about Jimmy's movements on the day his wife was murdered.'

When interviewed, former colleagues of Jimmy Livingstone's gave their own impressions. One person who worked as a messenger in taxes said of Jimmy: 'He knew we were beholden to him. He had the dishing out of overtime and treated men 20 years older than him like children. It was as if he was playing *Dad's Army*. He would line us up in the office after lunch, and march up and down saying, "I smell drink". We would stand there like gobshites, afraid to speak in case he would cut our overtime. He often had a gun in his drawer and would sometimes place it on the desk when he was reprimanding you.'

A female colleague who worked for him always got the impression that he never liked women. He was, in her opinion, a 'chauvinistic freak'.

'He would dress you down in his office and would not stop until he upset you so much that you started to cry. I was so upset about the way he treated me, I went to a colleague and said I was going to report him, but she advised against it, saying that if I did, he would make my life hell. I was not the least bit surprised to hear that, following his wife's murder, most of the female staff in his section would not work with him. Some even refused to place calls to him. What I remember most about my time working with him was that he was a total control freak.'

Senior personnel also shared this view. One inspector who worked with him said, 'Jimmy was extremely unpopular. He had given a lot of people a hard time, and as a result, there was very little support for him at the time of his wife's death. People were refusing to work with him and eventually we had to reassign his duties. Jimmy was always known as an aggressive individual and not only towards those at lower grades, but also those senior to him.'

***

Things were to get much worse for Jimmy Livingstone. In March 1993, Jimmy answered a knock at his front door. He was confronted by a number of Gardaí and detectives who arrested him under section 30 of the Offences Against the State Act. Jimmy found himself being handcuffed and taken from his house to a waiting Garda car for all his neighbours to see. He was brought to Swords Garda station and interviewed by seven sets of detectives over the next 48 hours. Eventually, he was released without charge, although he subsequently faced charges in respect to unlicensed firearms. Jimmy Livingstone claims that it was during this detention that he suffered most at the hands of Gardaí.

His first questioner allegedly asked Jimmy, 'Do you know why you are here, James? You are here because you killed your wife.' During the various interviews, Jimmy claims that he was subjected to numerous insults and that many attempts were made to intimidate him. He was also told he could spend up to a week in custody. Livingstone maintains that Gardaí told him lies in an attempt to undermine him. 'I was told that news of my arrest had been greeted with applause by my staff. It was also said to me that I would be sacked before the day was over.'

Jimmy was also told that his neighbours were elated with the news of his arrest. All of these claims were, according to Jimmy, totally inaccurate.

It was comments that were made about his relationship with Grace and his family that Jimmy says were most hurtful. While in custody he was told that the Gardaí were aware that he treated his wife like a slave, and he was also jeered that his son was a drug abuser, while other investigating Garda suggested that his daughter was a whore. Livingstone knew these were all tactics in an effort to break him. The final insult came when, during his last session, one of the detectives brought two of that day's newspapers into the room. Both carried stories about his arrest. 'The more sinister bit had yet to come,' says Jimmy. Jimmy claims: 'Wrapped in the newspaper, my inquisitor had colour photographs of Grace. These had probably been taken in the hospital where the post mortem had been performed. They were taken at various angles and showed Grace completely naked. I do not know the purpose of presenting these to me apart from whatever disturbing effect they were supposed to have on me. They did disturb me.'

Jimmy Livingstone knew that not only was he a suspect, but that he was the only one. Gardaí put it to him that he arrived home at about ten minutes to six. They suggested that when he got home his dinner was not ready, and while his wife was sweeping the floor he struck her. They claimed that he struck her too hard, and then in an effort to cover this up, he carried Grace upstairs and bound her. They maintain that he then went to his press, took out his shotgun and shot her. They claim that he only went to the neighbour in order to give him an alibi and not in an effort to save his wife. Jimmy describes this as preposterous, and also slams rumours that were spread at the time that his son Conor could have been involved in Grace's killing.

'A rumour went around that he [Conor] could have come out on a motorcycle and done it. For a start he never rode a motorcycle, to my knowledge he hasn't access to a motorcycle, and certainly a motorbike coming into our estate on that day would have attracted attention.'

Describing it as preposterous, Jimmy says it was in keeping with the other allegations being made against him. He is convinced that the killer murdered Grace in such a way as to frame him. He said that a very cold-blooded person had killed Grace and that it had been a very determined affair.

'From all the evidence and trail that was left behind, it would seem that it was done for the purpose of framing me. This, combined with the Garda axiom that 90 per cent of wives who are killed are killed by their husbands, constituted the Gardaí's case.'

Despite the pressure, the only charge that Jimmy Livingstone ever faced was one relating to the unlicensed firearms kept in his home. This is something that upset Cathal Cryan, who believed that Livingstone should have faced more serious charges.

'The DPP should not have prosecuted him for an unlicensed firearm in respect to the revolver. The fact is you cannot get a license for a revolver. He should have been charged with having a gun, which would lead to suspicion that it was held for unlawful purposes. Then let him explain why he had that gun. That charge under section 27 of the Firearms Act shifts the onus onto the accused. It is a far more serious charge and carries a long jail sentence upon conviction.'

Jimmy's interest in firearms was a justifiable cause of concern for the Gardaí. He readily admits that he used to carry the .45 revolver out of his home and use it for target practice. 'Conor and I would often go and shoot at tins and other targets with the .45.' While he saw no harm in this, it confirms that he did in fact take this illegal weapon from his home. This caused concern for more than one of Livingstone's neighbours, who were aware of his interest in firearms. In an interview following Grace's death, Jimmy admitted, 'Guns are part of my life. I don't tolerate anybody who abuses them, mind, but they help make a man a real man. I'm a macho man, I love shooting and the FCÁ, my boat and a few pints in the mess with the lads.'

There is no doubt that Jimmy Livingstone carried his guns about on his person, and that neighbours and colleagues were aware of this. Some were extremely frightened of him because of this love of guns; others simply put it down to his involvement in the FCÁ.

While Jimmy may have had a number of illegal weapons on the night his wife was murdered, he had also availed of the amnesty in 1972 which allowed people who held illegal firearms to turn them over to the army and therefore avoid prosecution. Cryan believed that the revolver was one of these guns. He maintains that this gun had been handed in at Griffith Barracks in the 1972 amnesty, and that Jimmy Livingstone then used his contacts in the army to have it transferred to McKee Barracks, where he was a commandant. Jimmy Livingstone confirms that he had a gun transferred, but says it was another handgun that he had transferred and not the .45 that was found at the house.

Cryan believes that bringing a .45 out in public, and carrying it about and using it for shooting practice in public areas is a total disregard for the law. Jimmy Livingstone sees no harm in this at all.

Cryan believes that he was right to consider Jimmy Livingstone a prime suspect in his wife's murder. He refers to his notes and says that he composed a list within days of Grace's body being found.

'In order for me to classify one a suspect in this case, one would have to test positive on any one of the following:

1. Access to the scene.
2. Opportunity.
3. Capacity to commit the crime.
4. Motive.
5. Conduct at time of report or discovery.
6. Access to a weapon and knowledge of same.
7. Ability to leave the scene undetected.
8. Proximity to the scene after the crime.
9. Evidence linking to the scene.
10. Evidence linking to the weapon.
11. Information and/or misinformation.
12. Conduct of a person in the hours, days and weeks after the crime.
13. General level of sanity.

'If a person tries to mislead you by suggesting that somebody else has committed the crime, that is good information. You can usually detect if somebody is planting information to direct you away from the truth.

'With the above list, if a person fails on any one criteria, then he must be considered a suspect. If he fails on six or more, then I would consider him a good suspect, and in light of the above, I was right to consider Jimmy Livingstone a very good suspect.'

However, for Cryan's theory to stand up, Grace Livingstone would have had to be murdered after Jimmy came home. While Cryan believes this is possible, it does not tie in with the opinions of experienced medical people at the scene. The doctor who attended Grace estimated that she had been dead for at least a number of hours. This was also the testimony of the ambulance driver who attended the scene and who has attended hundreds of such scenes in his career. He also estimated that the time of death was a number of hours before six. What is significant about the ambulance man's testimony is that it was included in his statement, as a detective who later read his statement said, 'I would not have allowed him to say that, I would never have included this in his statement.' Luckily for Jimmy Livingstone, another individual took the ambulance man's statement. Garda are not allowed to decide what should or should not be included in a person's statement on the basis of whether it suits their case.

Cryan dismisses these statements, pointing out that the only way to estimate the time of death is to take the temperature of the deceased, something that was not done on the night that Grace was killed.

'The woman [a nurse] who attended Grace also said that the body was warm when she arrived, and I did not take that into account either.'

Cryan knew from experience that both the nurse and ambulance driver were estimating the time of death, and that guessing on such a serious matter is dangerous in this kind of investigation. While the ambulance man's timing suited Jimmy Livingstone, the nurse's timing suited Cryan's theory, so he depended on neither.

Cryan believes that a windbreaker jacket that was in the house when detectives filmed the scene, but disappeared during the first few days of the investigation, is a crucial piece of evidence. According to Cryan, the only people who had access to the house were Jimmy Livingstone, who went to collect clothes, and Gardaí who were involved in the investigation.

Cryan accepts that errors were made on the part of the first investigating team: 'I accept that this jacket was crucial evidence, and what is more crucial is that it disappeared. This jacket could have been worn by the killer and had trace evidence linking it to the crime. This was also a waterproof type of jacket and as such could have protected the clothes of the killer. Unlike the Gardaí at the various tribunals, I accept we made mistakes. I have made mistakes in my career.'

Cryan believes that Jimmy Livingstone should never have been allowed back into the house on the day after the crime was committed. 'No one only Gardaí should have been allowed back into the house, as someone could have, knowingly or unknowingly, removed vital clues. This was a terrible mistake by the Gardaí.'

Jimmy Livingstone claims that the initial investigation team overlooked other vital evidence. When Jimmy returned to his home after the murder, he began to tidy the room where Grace had been found and alleges that he came across a syringe. He could not understand what this was doing there. 'I could not recall there ever having been a syringe in use in our home for any purpose. I was astounded that such an item should not have been discovered and not been the source of some enquiry from the supposed investigators.' Jimmy contacted the investigating team and advised them of his find.

'In due course, a detective called with a paper bag capable of holding 50 kilos of flour and took it away. This syringe was never mentioned to me afterwards.'

There was more important evidence overlooked according to Jimmy. A few weeks after the murder, he was out tending to his back garden when he made another discovery. 'I found a piece of stick in the shape of a conventional L-shaped walking stick,' he says. 'I did not remember having seen it before. I went to the outside door of the porch and inserted the stick through the letterbox with the stem first. Without any problem I was able to access the inside handle and open the door.'

Jimmy thought this was a significant find and immediately informed one of the investigating officers, Detective Inspector John Gallagher, and told him about the stick, offering to demonstrate for him how it worked. He pointed out that the murderer could have used this to gain access to the house. 'He showed no interest,' says Jimmy, 'I still have the stick.'

Some months after the murder, Jimmy claims he found shotgun cartridges behind the wardrobe where he stored his guns. 'These were not found by the many detectives who had access to my home for over four days following the murder, or by the other lot who searched my home on the day I was arrested. This is probably just another indication of the haphazard methods which were employed in that first investigation.' These too were handed over to investigating Gardaí.

***

As Jimmy Livingstone was of the view that the investigation was going nowhere, he decided to offer a substantial reward in an effort to find out who was responsible for Grace's murder. He decided to put up a reward of IR£50,000. It was hardly taken seriously by anybody he says, and some reporters seemed only interested in how he would raise the money. The offer of a reward did produce one interesting result however.

In June 1993, several months after the murder of Grace, a private detective telephoned Jimmy. The private detective explained that he knew someone who had information on the crime. He told Jimmy that he should meet this man, and a meeting was arranged for the same afternoon at the Green Isle Hotel on the Naas Road. Jimmy explains, 'By then I had such little faith in the capacity of the investigators that I could not see my way to confide in them.'

Jimmy had met this private detective through his time in the Revenue Commission and says that from his dealings with him, he was well aware that the private detective would be able to get information from a stratum of society alien to Jimmy himself. Jimmy set out to the Green Isle Hotel to meet both the private detective and his mysterious informer. He felt as if things might be changing for the better and hoped that a lead would be provided that would result in Grace's killer being convicted.

When they arrived at the hotel, the informant was anxious to discuss the reward. Jimmy studied the informer, and having observed hundreds of informers during his years in the Revenue, came to the view that the man was genuine. However, he insisted that no money would be paid until Grace's killer had been caught. This was agreed and the informer then said he needed to make some calls to other sources. His own phone was not working so Jimmy gave him his, and the informer made a total of four calls. After some small talk, the men parted, with the informant promising he would be in touch.

The next day Jimmy heard from the informant, who this time was alarmed and aggressive. The informant felt that Jimmy had tricked him into using his mobile phone the previous day so that he could see the numbers of the people he had called. He now feared that, because he had used Jimmy's phone, he was in danger of being exposed. Jimmy spoke to him, reassuring him that this was not the case. He eventually calmed him and persuaded him to try again to uncover the identity of Grace's killer. The informant said he would, but no further contact has ever been made.

***

There were to be many more bizarre twists as Jimmy went about trying to find the identity of Grace's killer. In 1997, when the Criminal Assets Bureau (CAB) searched the home of the alleged Dublin criminal known as the 'Monk', they found a videotape of Jimmy Livingstone. The recording showed clandestine footage of Jimmy meeting a source to try to uncover information concerning Grace's death. The first Jimmy knew of this was when he read it in the papers. Understandably intrigued, Jimmy arranged to meet the Monk. Their encounters were in the open in a hotel in North County Dublin, where they met on three separate occasions. But there was a further leak to the media from the Gardaí, and an article appeared quoting a CAB source, wrongly suggesting that Jimmy Livingstone was now acting as the Monk's unofficial tax advisor and was assisting him in his dealings with the CAB, which had served the Monk with a €2.5m tax demand.

***

Jimmy Livingstone kept up the pressure on the Gardaí, constantly berating them for failing to find Grace's killer. He continually demanded that action be taken, and called for a second enquiry into events of that day in December 1992. His persistence was rewarded in March 1994 when a second investigation was opened, which was headed up by now retired Superintendent Tom Connolly, and one of the state's most respected investigators, Inspector Todd O'Loughlin. However, this second investigation, has been strongly criticised by a number of those involved in the first investigation. Some of those critics are still serving and are reluctant to go on the record, but they share the view of retired

Detective Sergeant Cathal Cryan, who believes that the second investigation came about as a result of internal Garda politics. He maintains that the Gardaí were afraid of potential legal action by Livingstone. 'The Gardaí were afraid of Livingstone, he would always be roaring about the High Court and individual's tax affairs.'

Cryan is extremely critical of the *modus operandi* of the second team of investigators. 'I feel that maybe some of the officers involved in the second investigation may have had their minds made up before they started. They conducted that whole enquiry without contacting or speaking to any of us who were involved in the initial enquiry.' He believes that he was not contacted because it would have prevented the second investigation team from coming to the conclusion that they did. 'I know this case inside out and nobody on this planet could argue this case with me, they were afraid of that.'

The second investigation ran appeals on the RTÉ television programme *Crimeline*. This appeal produced a second witness, which was described as a major breakthrough in the case.

Cryan, however, saw it differently: 'This witness was brought into Malahide in a big fanfare with a blanket over his head to protect his identity. The investigators failed to run a check on him. If they had done so, they would have discovered that he also came forward to the first investigating team and we dismissed him. We had good reason to. At the time he was being investigated for a number of frauds by our own team, and we knew he was trying to ingratiate himself with the Gardaí.

'The witness told the second enquiry that [on the day of Grace Livingstone's murder] he had been sitting in the car park opposite the Stuart Hotel in Malahide, reading a newspaper. It was dark and there were no floodlights in the car park at the time. He told them, as he did us, that he drove from his home in Portmarnock to Malahide to buy the paper, which meant he passed three shops on the way. He said that between 4.30 and

4.50 pm, he saw two lads enter the car park and get into a chocolate-coloured fiesta. He was quite specific about the colour. None of his evidence checked out, yet it was used in subsequent reconstructions.

'This was not the first murder that this witness came forward in. He had also presented himself as a witness in a double murder that had occurred at the Rosnaree Hotel outside Drogheda. This was an INLA hit. He was also in a car park for that one and sighted a suspicious car on that occasion also.'

Cryan also dismisses other findings of the second enquiry as totally flawed and unreliable. On Wednesday, 16 March, 1994, six policemen called to the home of Jimmy Livingstone. This time the call was by arrangement. It was now 15 months after Grace's murder and a year since Jimmy had been branded the prime suspect. A series of basic policing operations was about to begin. The team of six split up, with guards positioning themselves in neighbouring houses. During the first investigation, reports had been made of a loud noise heard in the estate around 4.30 pm on the day that Grace was shot. The Gardaí involved in the first investigation satisfied themselves that this noise had come from a crew working on behalf of TV cable providers NTL. However, the second investigation were not fully satisfied with this explanation and decided that this noise could have been the echo of a gunshot. If this were the case, then it would help to establish the time of death and would also remove suspicion away from Jimmy Livingstone.

Cryan, however, dismisses the results. 'On 16 March, the second investigation carried out a so-called reconstruction test, overseen by a prime suspect. I mean where in the name of God or on what planet would such a test be carried out? Naturally I had an interest in the findings, and although I was not involved, I had a good source who was keeping me informed of what was happening.

'At 7.50 that night I received a phone call to say the test was negative, but that being the case, they were going to carry it out again the following week. When they carried out the second test, they opened the windows [in Livingstone's house], even though the windows were not opened on the day of the murder.'

Another detective who does not want to be identified as he is still a member of the force said: 'All we were short of doing was going onto the road and discharging the shots until they were heard. I know that the second investigation did not set about to solve this crime, but set out to undermine the first investigation. This is the first time that I am aware of, that as a result of pressure from a suspect we set out to come up with a time and scenario for a crime.'

The other piece of vital evidence that the second investigation turned up was an unidentified finger mark on the tape that was used to tie Grace. It was never publicly disclosed to whom this belonged.

Cryan explains it as follows: 'When evidence was taken from the house to the bureau, there was a ball of binding tape. This is the tape that was used to tie Grace. Some weeks later the results came through, and it was disclosed that there was an unidentified mark on the tape. We were asked to gather up the innocent prints, that is all the people who had access to the scene or the remains, people like ambulance drivers, medics and so on. It was important to eliminate these people. I completed this task with one of my main allies in this investigation, Mick McGuire, now deceased. We had to go back and take 39 sets of prints, and when these were sent into the bureau, we were asked to recheck one set of prints. Before they told us who they wanted checked, I said to them I know who it is, and when I named the person they said I was correct. This was an ambulance driver who accidentally picked up the tape. I witnessed him pick up the tape at the scene, and the unidentified mark was found in the middle of the tape, which indicated that it was lifted between the finger and thumb as it was examined.'

Those involved in the second investigation say that there is no way Jimmy Livingstone could have been responsible for his wife's killing. They are adamant that the timing makes it impossible. They even ran a reconstruction on *Crimeline* which clearly stated that they were looking for other suspects.

The members of the second investigation team satisfied themselves that the time of death was about 4.30 pm, largely based on the fact that a number of neighbours claimed that they had heard a loud noise that day around this time.

The first team has statements that state that Grace's car was parked on the roadway at 4.40 pm. Other statements say that the car was moved to the driveway shortly before 5 pm. When the house was inspected, Grace's keys were found in the normal place. Those involved in the initial investigation consider it most unlikely that Grace's murderer commited the crime at 4.30 pm and then decided to move Grace's car and place the keys back in their normal place.

Jimmy Livingstone believes that the second Garda investigation into the case, which overturned the original detectives' belief that he was his wife's killer, has quietly faded. 'I should be pleased that the second investigation team were as competent and professional as they were,' says Jimmy. However, he regrets the fact that they never completed the job by finding the killer. Jimmy believes that a mountain of evidence exists and that substantial clues still need to be followed up, yet little is being done.

On the day in March when the noise tests were being carried out by the second investigation team and the results were suggesting Jimmy's innocence, Jimmy was hoping for far more. He quotes a newspaper story that appeared when news of the second investigation broke, and says the comments remain with him now.

'There must be some public disquiet that it has taken so long for an internal Garda review to conclude James Livingstone could not have killed his wife ... Both Mr Livingstone and the public deserve better.'

Years since the trail went cold, question marks still hang over the Garda file on the Grace Livingstone case. A murdered woman's widower has faced loss, accusation, deceit and finally enforced ignorance.

Jimmy Livingstone no longer lives in the house where this awful crime occurred. He chose to leave the memories behind him and has moved to a smaller home within walking distance of Malahide village. He has left behind neighbours, many of whom always supported him and believed he was the victim of two tragedies: the first being the murder of his wife and the second the way he was victimised and harassed by a group of Gardaí who contended that he had committed this heinous crime.

But Jimmy Livingstone was never a man to lie down and accept defeat. He feels he was wronged and still has faith in some aspects of the justice system. Jimmy, his daughter Tara, and his son Conor issued proceedings against the Minister for Justice, Ireland and the Attorney General in 1995. The Gardaí are facing yet another potential scandal as they are being sued for false imprisonment, abuse of legal process, conspiracy, slander and negligence.

This is a case which will catch the public's imagination, a case which the Livingstone family have waited eight years to be heard and a case which they hope will go some way to establishing the wrongdoing they allege was perpetrated against them. It has been a long-drawn-out case, but in 2004, Jimmy won an important victory: Gardaí were ordered to hand files over to him to allow him to proceed with his civil action. There are serious allegations being made against the Gardaí, and if what has been alleged by way of affidavit is proven in court, then the Gardaí face a scandal as damaging to the force as any that has gone before.

Just months after the killing, Jimmy told a newspaper: 'What upsets me more than anything is that Grace isn't here, all the wrong that has happened to me, the hurt that those gobshites are pouring on me, but so what? None of it brings Grace back, that's all that matters, she's gone. They can't take away the life we've had.'

2

Philip Cairns

Many people have gone missing in Ireland over the years. One of the most high-profile of these was Philip Cairns.

Philip Cairns lived in Rathfarnham in south Dublin, and was 13 years of age when he went missing in 1986. He features on many missing persons websites, he has been written about in numerous books, and he has even been the subject of a TV programme that tried to trace his last movements. Every year there are articles written in the papers about him, and yet his case still remains unsolved.

Philip's disappearance is described as one of the most baffling missing person's cases that has ever been investigated by the Gardaí. At the time Philip disappeared, he was 5 feet 2 inches tall, with brown hair and hazel eyes. He had a small birthmark under his chin. Philip was a deeply religious boy who lived at home with his parents, four older sisters and one younger brother. Those who knew him describe him as a shy, sensitive and kind young man, who did not involve himself in many of the normal interests shared by his peers.

At lunchtime on Thursday, 23 October, 1986, Philip Cairns was having what would be his last lunch at home. As he ate, he finished off the homework that was to be handed up that afternoon. Philip lived just a 15-minute walk away from his school, Coláiste Éanna. This suited him well as it allowed him 30 minutes at home each lunchtime.

On this particular day, Philip had his lunch with his granny, Mae, who was living with the Cairns family at the time. They were not alone at home, however, as Philip's mother, Alice, was upstairs getting ready to go to town, where one of her other children, her daughter Helen, had a dental appointment. Philip's sister Suzanne was also home at the time.

It was a normal day in the Cairns household, and as Philip finished off his work, he packed his canvas school bag with the books he required for his afternoon classes. He called goodbye to his granny and left the house. It was about 1.30 pm when Philip started out on his walk to school. Philip's house is on the busy Ballyroan Road in Rathfarnham, where there is a constant flow of traffic. It was a bright day, but being the middle of September, Philip wore a bomber jacket over his school uniform. He appeared to be in good form as he headed back to school, but at some stage someone intervened, and Philip never made it back to his classes that day.

It would be many hours before people would become aware that, within minutes of his leaving home, Philip Cairns had gone missing. The fact that he did not return to school that afternoon is not necessarily something that would cause concern for either his teachers or fellow students. It was normal enough for a student to remain at home for an afternoon. There was the possibility that he had felt unwell and his mother had told him to take the afternoon off. The school year had begun six weeks earlier, and there were many new classes to attend. There was no reason that his absence from class would be a cause of concern for the three teachers he was to have had that afternoon. As Philip was a good student, no one suspected that he may be skipping classes. School finished as normal, but as the evening wore on, there was no sign of Philip returning to his home.

It was not normal for Philip to be late home. In fact, it was totally out of character as he was an extremely dependable young lad. However, when his father, who is also called Philip, arrived home from his day's work, he was not too concerned when he heard that Philip had not returned home from school. Although it was out of character, his father was aware that Philip had met new friends in secondary school, and thought that he might be with them in his new surroundings at Coláiste Éanna.

When Philip's mother Alice returned from town, however, and her daughter told her that Philip had not returned home from school, she knew straight away that something was wrong and she immediately became worried and concerned. She decided to call to the home of Philip's closest friend, Enda Cloke, to see if Philip was there. Enda told Alice that he had no idea where Philip might be, and that he had not seen him all day. Alice then contacted the school, where a teacher informed her that Philip had not been back to school at all that afternoon. Suddenly everyone realised that something was very wrong, Philip Cairns was missing.

On hearing that Philip had not been to school that afternoon, Alice returned to Enda Cloke's house and spoke with his father Paddy. As Paddy was a garda, she felt he would know what to do. Paddy immediately contacted Rathfarnham Garda station, informing them that Philip was missing. When the Gardaí became aware of what sort of a child Philip was, when they learned how dependable he was, they decided something was very wrong. Shortly after the initial phone call, a garda called to the Cairns house for a picture of Philip. The search had begun.

The following morning, a detective inspector called to the Cairns home and told Philip's parents that because Philip was usually a reliable, well-behaved child, and because of the bad weather conditions the previous night, they accepted that this was not just a case of a child wandering off. He informed the family that they would not wait the normal 48 hours before launching a major investigation into Philip's disappearance. All stations around the city, and particularly those in neighbouring districts, were put on full alert. Pictures of Philip were circulated to various stations and an incident room was set up. Some detectives were already beginning to fear the worst. They knew that his disappearance had not been reported until a full eight hours after it occured and therefore the abductors had that much headstart on them. It had also taken a further 12 hours before a proper investigation had begun. This would surely make the case more difficult for them to solve.

It seemed strange that a teenage boy could simply vanish off the face of the earth. The fact that Philip disappeared so close to his home and in the middle of the day shocked people. Residents in the Rathfarnham and neighbouring areas were concerned that Philip's attackers might strike again. Parents were rightly worried for their own children's safety, as search after search failed to produce any clues, and the investigating officers had absolutely no idea what had happened to Philip.

All that was known was that 13-year-old Philip Cairns had been abducted shortly after he left his home to return to school. One garda who worked on the case believes that Philip was most likely lifted within a few yards of his home. 'The fact that no one saw Philip walk along the road or saw him get into a car leads me to believe that he was literally seconds on the road. We spoke to many people who travelled the road that day, and no one saw any sign of Philip. This in itself is most unusual and indicated that he was only on the road for a very short period of time. It would appear that Philip's abductors were waiting for him to leave his house.'

***

There have been many theories about what may have happened to Philip Cairns, but the truth is that while the case remains unsolved, no one actually knows what occurred on that awful day in October. What is known is that there was no struggle witnessed, there were no strange cars seen in the area, and there were no screams heard. This lack of evidence would indicate that Philip knew his abductor well and was happy to accept the offer of a lift back to school.

The Headmaster from his national school, Mr Flynn, who had known Philip for six years before his disappearance, is adamant that Philip would not have accepted a lift from a stranger. In an interview some time after Philip's abduction, he said, 'It wasn't in his nature to rush over to a car if somebody was asking for directions ... I could not see him crossing the road or even going as far as the kerb if somebody was asking for directions ... I would say that he wouldn't get into somebody's car or van or bus without knowing who they were.'

It was also the belief of Philip's aunt, Terry Moore, that a person known to Philip had abducted him. She said that Philip would not have got into a car belonging to someone he did not know. She added that Philip would only have got into a car with someone he trusted, and she raised the possibility that it could be someone close to the immediate family.

The week following his disappearance, it was reported in one paper that Philip may have been the subject of bullying, and that this could have caused him to run away or mitch school. This suggestion was based on a number of reports to Gardaí that older pupils were bullying Philip at school. A number of Philip's classmates told the investigating Gardaí that this was happening, and it was soon confirmed. Gardaí felt that Philip would have been an easy target for the bullies because of his gentle manner and his strong religious beliefs. After having discussions with teachers and pupils, Gardaí satisfied themselves that it was no more than boisterous behaviour and that it was normal for first-year pupils to be joked with. Being more sensitive than most other boys, Philip took it more seriously, but it was felt that it did not concern him enough to cause him to run away.

Philip's disappearance was widely reported in the media, and as a result, hundreds of people, including neighbours and civil defence members, joined the Cairns family and the Gardaí in the search. This display of goodwill from neighbours and friends, as well as hundreds of people who did not know Philip, was a great source of comfort to the Cairns family. But the family also had to endure the cranks that are sick enough to take pleasure in others people's pain. In the week after his abduction, many calls were made to the Cairns home. Some of these were made by people claiming that they had Philip with them and that he would be soon returning home.

The national school that Philip had attended went on mid-term break the day he was abducted, and a week later, when they returned to school, the Headmaster, Mr Flynn, who had been away for the week, called to see how the Cairns family were coping with this terrible crisis. As Mr Flynn was leaving the Cairns' home after his visit, the phone rang. Mrs Cairns' sister took the phone call and an anonymous caller told her that Philip's body could be found in a river at the back of his old school.

Even though he knew the message was most likely another red herring, one of many that were enraging people, when Mr Flynn returned to the school grounds he found himself going to the back of the school as described and making his way to the river. As he was looking into the river, a person jumped up in the water and nearly gave Mr Flynn a heart attack. It was a Garda sub aqua diver who, as part of the ongoing investigation, was searching in the river for Philip. Mr Flynn did not know they were carrying out searches in the river at the time.

***

The fact that Phipip had not been sighted, nor a body found, since his disappearance makes this only the second such case in Ireland in a long number of years. The other was six-year-old Mary Boyle, who went missing in Donegal in March 1977. Mary was last seen following her uncle to a neighbour's house, and when Mary vanished, her uncle assumed she had returned home. Mary Boyle has not been seen since.

Although many minors went missing in England and Scotland during these years, this was not the case in Ireland. Philip was the only minor to go missing in Ireland in 1986, compared to 810 under the age of 14 in the greater London area. In 1986, 1000 people in Ireland were reported missing and this number rises every year. Most of the files are closed within days, however, as people return home or are discovered living somewhere else. Of all the cases reported in 1986, only 14 remained missing at the end of that year.

Statistics are no comfort to an affected family. The pain suffered by those who loved Philip cannot be imagined by any of us who have not experienced such a loss. As the days went by, it was becoming more and more difficult for the Cairns family. Why were there no clues? Why were there no witnesses? And most importantly, why was there no sign of Philip? So many questions, yet so few answers.

***

One week after his disappearance, in an effort to progress the investigation, detectives involved in the search for Philip called a meeting in his school. Although Philip's fellow students were on their mid-term break, they were anxious to help, as were their parents, who were still frightened for the safety of children in the area, and the teachers, who were baffled and also concerned for Philip's safety. The fact that there was no sign led many to believe the worst. Gardaí attempted to jog someone's memory or glean some small piece of information which could lead to them solving this case.

The meeting went well. Gardaí were satisfied that, even though the children were nervous, they had been able to establish a relationship with them. They were confident that if any person connected to the school had information, they would come forward.

Then, within hours, Gardaí thought they had their first major breakthrough. It was a wet evening, and at about 7.30 pm two teenage girls were walking through a laneway just a few hundred yards from Philip's home when they came across a school bag. They picked up the bag, and when they examined the contents, they discovered that it contained the school books of Philip Cairns. The girls immediately went to Rathfarnham Garda station and handed the bag to a detective involved with the case. The bag was relatively dry even though it had been raining. Gardaí concluded that it had been placed there no more than an hour or two before the girls found it. The lane where the bag was found had already been searched by Gardaí, and they were satisfied that it had not been there earlier. 'It could not have been missed,' said one officer who had been involved in the original investigation.

News of the find was passed to the Cairns family, and it is said that one over-enthusiastic Garda told them that Philip was in the area and would be home soon. Unfortunately, their hopes were short lived as there was no sign of Philip. The discovery of the bag proved to be more of a distraction than a help, in that it caused a lot of rumour about its origin.

Some books had been removed from the bag, including a religious book, which caused people to speculate that Philip had been kidnapped by some religious cult. Detectives visited some known cults in the greater Dublin area to check out the remote possibility that Philip was being held against his will. The only thing the Gardaí learned was that none of the cults were a cause for concern. The people they spoke to were horrified that they would be considered suspects in such a terrible act.

The fact that no one ever came forward with information on the bag has been a cause of major frustration for investigating Gardaí down the years. The widely held belief is that when the children attended the school meeting earlier that day and listened to the appeals from the investigating Gardaí for information, one child, who had found Philip's bag and kept it, became afraid. It is thought that following the meeting this child went to a part of the lane where he or she could not be seen and placed Philip's bag there.

At the time of the find, Philip's father told one paper, 'When they found the school bag we were all so relieved. We were convinced he was on his way home and would be here within a matter of minutes, so we all went out looking for him.'

One garda who worked on the original investigation said, 'I always believed that the bag was placed there by a child who had come across it on the day Philip was abducted, and took the bag home with him or her. He or she then became too afraid to admit he or she had the bag, but had he or she admitted this to us and pointed out where he or she originally found Philip's schoolbag, it may have given us a better picture of what occurred at the time Philip was abducted. I can understand that person being frightened at the time, but now he or she is an adult and should realise the importance of coming forward and telling us all he or she knows about the bag.'

However, not all of those who worked on the investigation share this view. One officer, who has since retired, said he believes that the bag was deliberately placed there by Philip's abductors to create hope and chaos. He maintains that had a child been worried about finding and taking Philip's bag, they would have spoken to their parents, who would have sorted it out for them and dealt with the Gardaí on the matter. He also believes that if a child had been responsible for this, he would have told another child and soon this information would have filtered back to the investigation team.

'The fact that his bag was found in a laneway which is used regularly makes me wonder if it was placed there in a deliberate attempt to mislead the investigation and the public. Were the religious books taken because the people who were responsible for Philip's abduction knew of his and his family's strong faith? If this was the purpose of placing the bag, then it worked. For days and even weeks there were stories and wild speculation because the books were gone. There were ridiculous stories saying that religious cults kidnapped him, and that he was being held in a place and brainwashed. I am sure that the people who placed the bag there knew exactly what they were doing. These are undoubtedly very clever people.'

***

While many journalists, detectives and members of the public have speculated about what may have happened to Philip in the years since his disappearance, there is one theory that seems to be accepted as being the closest to the truth. That is that young Philip Cairns did not run away or leave his family of his own free will, rather he was abducted.

The question then remains: why did Philip's attackers feel it was necessary to make him disappear? One explanation is that Philip was being sexually abused. It is known that a number of paedophiles were operating in the Rathfarnham area at the time of his disappearance, and it is possible that some of these were abusing him. It has also been suggested by many people close to the Cairns family that Philip's attacker was well known to his family. Paedophiles are known to not only befriend the children they abuse, but in most cases the family of the victim as well.

In 1997, a man widely regarded in Republican circles, and well known for the endless work he did on behalf of abused children (let us call him Mr X), is said to have become aware that a man (let us call him Mr Y) had admitted during interrogation by hard-line

Republicans that he had been involved in the abduction of Philip Cairns. Republicans had become aware of Mr Y's involvement in the crime because he had been talking loosely while drunk one evening when in the company of an individual who had links to Republicans.

Mr X claimed that when he became aware of this admission, he approached the Gardaí. He offered to set Mr Y up so that he could be recorded admitting to his part in Philip's abduction and perhaps also identifying the others who were responsible for Philip's murder. He claims, however, that this offer was never taken up. This is not the only evidence allegedly offered to the Gardaí that was never followed up.

Some people believe that when Philip began attending Coláiste Éanna, and became friendly with other children of his age who had not known him in junior school, he realised that the abuse that he had been suffering was wrong. Some believe that as a result of what he learned in school, and from what other students told him, Philip realised that he should tell someone what was happening. It was said by Mr Y that Philip had wrestled with his conscience. Mr Y suggested that Philip had then spoken to a person involved with the Church, seeking guidance, he was going to expose the abuse.

It is possible that without realising it, Philip had spoken to a person who was also abusing children, and was also perhaps part of a paedophile ring that was suspected to be operating in the Rathfarnham area. Unwittingly, Philip may have signed his own death warrant. It may have been that in order for this person to protect himself and the people who were abusing Philip, it was decided that it would be necessary to kidnap and murder Philip.

As Philip was leaving his house to go back to school, he had no reason to suspect that he was about to be abducted. The fact that there was no evidence of a struggle suggests that Philip was approached by a person well known to him and was offered a lift back to school. Philip would have done what most people would do in that situation and accepted the lift. According to My Y's confession, Philip was overpowered while in the car and then driven to a location in the Tallaght area. When it was safe, he was transferred to a van. The driver went about the rest of his day's business and later that night Philip's young body was dumped in a pond in the grounds of the Loreto Abbey, Rathfarnham, a few miles from his home.

A number of Gardaí who were involved with the investigation suspected that Philip had been murdered and some believed that he might have been dumped in a pond. Shortly after Philip's disappearance, as part of the investigation, a number of ponds in Blessington and the Phoenix Park were searched, but the ponds in the grounds of Loreto Abbey Convent were not. Subsequent statements by Gardaí say these were searched, but a number of gardaí involved at the time admitted that the ponds in the Loreto Abbey Convent grounds were overlooked.

I became aware of these claims in October 2002, and when I investigated further, I was able to establish that Mr X was indeed well known in Republican circles, and that he was regarded as extremely reliable. Mr X was not a person known to make up such stories and he certainly had access to the intelligence that was gathered by various Republican groups. I reported this in the *Sunday Independent* in November 2002.

Subsequent reports in another newspaper claimed that there had never been any ponds in the Loreto Abbey grounds, but this is untrue. According to one maintenance man who worked at the abbey, contractors moved thousands of tons of filling into the grounds and covered over one such pond in the early to mid-1980s. A retirement home for nuns was then built on this site. Another pond in the grounds was part of reclaimed land that was used for tennis courts.

When I wrote about this story for the *Sunday Independent*, members of Philip's extended family asked to meet me. When we met in a hotel in Portlaoise, they told me that all along they had believed that Philip had been abducted and murdered by a paedophile who had befriended the Cairns family. It was not only members of Philip's extended family who believed that a paedophile had abducted Philip; his father confirmed to me in an interview at his home that he believed a paedophile was responsible for his son's death. He said that he often worries more about what Philip may have suffered prior to his death than the actual murder itself.

Mr Cairns also expressed concern about an incident in June 2002 involving a man and a child in the area where Philip disappeared. On that occasion, a boy was allegedly approached and asked to get into the man's car. The boy refused and told his parents about the incident that night. The Gardaí never made the incident public because nothing had happened and nobody had seen anything. When I interviewed Mr Cairns for the *Sunday Independent*, he suggested that it was the same person who had abducted Philip. Whatever about a paedophile ring, Mr Cairns is of the view that a paedophile was involved in the abduction of his son.

Various detectives who have been involved with the investigation over the years share this view. One who worked on the earlier part of the investigation told me, 'After a few days we knew that Philip had been kidnapped. It was not until some time afterwards that we realised that more than one person must have been involved in his abduction. A number of people who we would have regarded as perverts were visited by us, but this produced no results. However, if these rings, which operate with more secrecy that the masons or the knights, were responsible, then it is no wonder we never found Philip.

'There were rumours about people at the time and these were all checked out, the investigation was classed as a missing person, but everyone knew soon after his disappearance that we were looking for a body and that we were in fact investigating a murder, without any evidence of the crime having been committed.'

***

A teacher who taught Philip for two years in national school and who later became Headmaster of the school, Mr Gerry O'Brien, believes that someone who Philip met through his prayer group or church-related activities was responsible for Philip's disappearance and subsequent death.

In an interview in 1994, Mr O'Brien told one journalist, 'I gave many, many hours just thinking about it, because it was unbelievable. It was mind boggling for us to think that one of our lads who could have been anybody's son or daughter, could go missing in broad daylight on the Ballyroan Road. Then there was not as much traffic, but there was still a flow of traffic, it was a busy road always. The only thing that made any sense to me, and I tried to figure out every angle, would be something like this. What would lure Philip away? If he had met you somewhere in a prayer group or in the church context, and you were a dried-out alcoholic, and you said to him, "Philip, I am tempted to go back on the drink, would you meet me and say a prayer with me some time, just you and me, just for a couple of minutes, say sometime after lunch. I'll meet you in Ann Devlin Park, but don't say anything; I don't want anyone to know I am tempted to go back on the beer." An angle like that Philip would take at face value. To a normal kid who had no particular interest in religion, that might seem odd, he might say come off it. But Philip, given his interest in religion and his belief that prayer was important, and the way he was reared, it would have made some sense to him, because I would say they were used to saying prayers at home. Someone asking him to say a prayer would not be as far-fetched as maybe asking a kid who never thought about religion.'

This shows that the man who taught Philip for two years before his abduction thinks that Philip was possibly tricked into meeting a person known to him who wanted to have him removed from society. Why would a person want to do this? What would be his motive? There is no doubt that a lot of planning went into the circumstances surrounding Philip's disappearance. His abduction was planned with military precision, or else some clue would have been left, some error made and something would have eventually turned up following the long and exhaustive enquiry that was carried out at the time by the Gardaí.

One evening, many years after Philip disappeared, a fund-raising auction was held in Philip's former national school. One parent who had developed an interest in Philip's case because he feared for his own children's safety, attended in the hope of obtaining some information that would indicate what might have happened to Philip on the day he disappeared. This man met one of the teachers from the school, who he found to be very forthcoming about Philip's case. The teacher told this parent that he thought that Philip's disappearance could have been organised by a religious cult, and that he had knowledge that Philip had being writing to one such cult in Australia prior to his disappearance. There is absolutely no evidence that Philip was writing to an Australian cult. Philip's parents confirmed to this parent that they had no knowledge of any such thing happening. The parent also claims that the teacher told him that it was he who had pointed the investigation toward the religious cult theory. It is hard to understand why a teacher would take this course of action without any proof that the theory were true.

The rumour that religious groups abducted Philip led to many far-fetched stories being circulated, and this undoubtedly caused unnecessary pain for the Cairns family. The fact that they were a religious family was used to create a smokescreen around Philip's disappearance. Some people suggested that the fact that Philip's mother was a member of a prayer group and was regularly at prayer meetings was in some way related to Philip's disappearance.

The former Headmaster of the national school, Mr Flynn, is, like his colleague Gerry O'Brien, adamant that Philip knew his attackers and would not have taken a lift from a stranger. In an interview some years later, Mr Flynn said, 'It was not somebody driving along, putting on the brakes and saying "Hey you". He picked the wrong guy, because he [Philip] would be too cool, too relaxed to just take off like that. Was it somebody he knew? It was, as a matter of fact.'

Mr Flynn was also critical of the Garda investigation at the time that Philip disappeared. He felt that there was too much concentration on the secondary school, where Philip had been a pupil for just six weeks. He felt more emphasis should have been placed on the junior school.

'It wasn't the centre of a thorough investigation and never was at any stage ... If I was a garda, I would have first of all checked out all the staff because you would have to think that maybe there was a particular relationship there ... I would have checked out the children to see if they were missing on the day or if they were in the vicinity.' Mr Flynn also stated that neither he nor any of the staff in the junior school were asked to give a statement to the police at the time of Philip's abduction.

***

One man who believes that Philip was attacked and murdered by a paedophile ring is 63-year-old James Connolly from The Ward in Co. Dublin. In 1991, while taking his usual evening walk, Mr Connolly started to think about Philip and his plight, and decided that he would try to find out what had happened to the boy. Mr Connolly has since spent many long hours in search of the truth. He has always felt that the fact that there has never been closure for the Cairns family is a tragedy.

In 1994, Mr Connolly offered a reward of IR£20,000 for information that would help to find Philip or to establish what had happened to him on the day of his abduction. He placed the reward money with his solicitor, and set up a confidential phone line. Telecom Eireann supplied this line free of charge when they heard that Mr Connolly was trying to help solve the Philip Cairns case.

One of the callers to this line claimed that he had been told that another boy from Philip's class in junior school had also been the victim of sexual abuse. If verified, this information could have been a major breakthrough in the case. Finding someone who had abused children in Philip's class could have brought an end to some of the suffering being experienced by the Cairns family. If a victim of child abuse could be identified and if it could be proven that the same person who committed this crime had also abused Philip, then the Gardaí would have the clue they had sought for so many years. There were other callers to this phone line who also gave information that had not been investigated before.

James Connolly felt that he was making ground and immediately informed the Gardaí at Rathfarnham Garda station of the existence of tapes of these confidential phone calls and the information they contained. For the first time since he had set about trying to establish what had happened to Philip, he really believed that there could be an end in sight. He felt that when the Gardaí listened to the tapes, they might come across something new which would assist the investigation. Mr Connolly offered to hand over the tapes immediately, but it would be a further nine years before Gardaí would hear the tapes and their content. Mr Connolly was totally confused by their reaction, and felt that they were not taking him seriously. It was, he says, not until a story appeared in the *Sunday Independent* about the existence of the tapes that the Gardaí got in touch. That was nine years after he had first offered them to the investigating team.

Mr Connolly also came into possession of taped interviews between a journalist and some of the teaching staff at Philip's national school. These had been recorded in 1992, but the Gardaí investigating the case had not heard these either. It must be said that the current investigators were anxious to hear these tapes as soon as they learned of their existence.

When I wrote a story for the *Sunday Independent* about the existence of the tapes and revealed that the teaching staff had given these interviews some 11 years earlier, I was asked to hand these over to the investigators. They have since been examined and any leads that may have arisen from them have been fully investigated. Garda sources close to the current investigation have informed me that as a result of these tapes, a member of staff from the junior school at the time that Philip attended was interviewed in 2003 concerning their content.

***

In 2002, a man contacted the Gardaí and told him that he wanted to confess to the murder of Philip Cairns. When the name Philip Cairns was mentioned, the operator immediately paid attention. The call was taped and passed over to Rathfarnham Gardaí. The background noise led them to believe that the phone used for the call was located in a public house, but when it was traced, it belonged to a private residence in the city centre. When Gardaí visited this residence, the occupants were shocked to learn that their phone had been used, and denied all knowledge of the call. This proved to be another dead end for the investigators.

While there is no actual evidence that Philip was murdered, those close to the case and those who have investigated it have formed the view that he was definitely murdered. The problem is, however, that in cases such as this, people are often afraid to say what they really believe because when a person is classified as missing, there is still a glimmer of hope for those left behind. There is also no definite motive for Philip's abduction or killing. Indeed, if there were, then there would probably be a suspect.

Subsequent events and what we have learned about child abuse in the years since Philip's disappearance have made his case easier to understand. Some days after Philip disappeared, Derry O'Rourke, who lived on the same road as Philip, moved out of his home. O'Rourke was a swimming instructor who was subsequently convicted of child abuse and is currently serving a prison sentence for his serious abuse of children over a period of 20 years. His first known offence took place in the early 1970s and his behaviour continued until 1992 when he was sentenced for his crimes.

Another man in the Rathfarnham area, who cannot be named in order to protect his victims, was convicted of raping his nephew and is currently serving a life sentence for various sexual assaults on young boys. He admitted to a number of sexual assaults on children between 1989 and 2000. He was also convicted of taking pornographic images of young children in the bedroom of his home during the same period. Therefore, despite the dismissal by various reporters of the existence of a paedophile ring operating in Rathfarnham at the time of Philips disappearance, it is an established fact that there was a lot of paedophile activity going on.

Operation Amethyst has shown us that hundreds of people from all walks of life in Ireland partake in paedophile activity. Operation Amethyst was one of the biggest Garda operations ever carried out in this country. Over 500 officers took part in synchronised raids, which involved almost every Garda division in the country. On the morning and afternoon of Monday, 27 May, 2002, more than 100 searches were carried out in homes, businesses and offices. Among the homes raided were those of a judge, a barrister, solicitors, the owner of a children's fun park, school headmasters, a librarian, a banker, a choir master, a health board official and the chief executive of a large company.

Gardaí were acting on information provided by the FBI in the US through Interpol. In 1999, the FBI ordered a massive surveillance investigation into Internet child pornography following information supplied to it from the United States Postal Service (USPS). The FBI surveillance operation logged 150,000 suspects across the world who had allegedly purchased material from an Internet site. Details of some 130 of these suspects were passed on to Gardaí. The inquiries centred on the alleged use of credit cards to acquire pornographic material over the Internet.

Gardaí say there was no concrete evidence of a paedophile ring operating in the Rathfarnham area at the time of Philip's disappearance, but the fact that there was no evidence found does not mean it did not exist.

None of the articles or books that I have read on the case of Philip Cairns have mentioned the fact that people came forward with information that the Gardaí never followed up. None of the articles ever mentioned the fact that teachers who taught Philip were not interviewed. It is not enough to record how Philip went missing and how his loved ones are suffering because there is no closure in his case. We must question what has been done, what is being done and what needs to be done to try and solve the mystery of Philip's disappearance, which has baffled so many for so long.

Those honest enough to admit it accept that Philip Cairns is dead, yet there has never been a murder enquiry. There is no body so there is no evidence of a murder to investigate. Philip's family has been denied closure as they have not been afforded the opportunity to bury their son. Philip was a child who was cruelly taken from a loving family and then had his life taken from him. Philip was a boy who supported those weaker than himself; he had strong faith and only saw good in people. He became an easy target for those who wanted to exploit his kindness. The reality is that only those responsible for his abduction really know what happened to Philip, and unless his remains are found, we may never learn what happened to this kind young boy who had his full life ahead of him. If there is one thing worse than the certainty of death, it is not knowing what has happened to a love one and the false hope involved, with no chance to properly grieve one's loss. If ever a section of society is denied justice, it is those families who have a loved one missing.

***

The disappearance of Philip Cairns shocked the country. Today in modern Ireland, the disappearance of Philip Cairns would not receive the same coverage, because the reality is that today many young people go missing and never return. Their names do not stand out like Philip Cairns, not because they are less important, but because we have become more complacent.

In Ireland, thousands of people are reported missing each year. There are many different types of missing persons: those who wanted to leave of their own free will, without telling anyone close to them; those who decide to take their own lives, but because their bodies are not found, are still classed as missing persons; and those who have been abducted and murdered. All cases are classed as missing persons until a body has been found.

Some who have been murdered may be the victims of a serial killer, an idea that was the subject of much speculation in the late 1990s and which some of the Gardaí's most experienced investigators still believe. Then there are the victims of gangland killing. Criminals know that as long as there is no body, no big investigation takes place, so when they want to eliminate someone who has not paid for a drug deal or who has crossed one of the many crime bosses in the country, they kill him or her and hide the body. While these people are soon reported as missing, many know that in reality they have been murdered.

While researching the stories of people who are missing in Ireland for an article in the *Sunday Independent*, I met Father Aquinas Duffy, who is based in Tallaght. Father Aquinas is responsible for setting up the missing persons website in Ireland. He did this when his nephew Aengus (Gussie) Shanahan went missing in Limerick in February 2000. In an effort to locate his nephew and to help his family, Father Aquinas set up a web site where he posted details of his nephew. He found himself inundated with calls from people who were also looking for missing loved ones. He was asked to include their details on his site and now the site is visited by tens of thousands of people each year who are searching for missing people.

Father Aquinas is one of the best informed in the area of missing people in Ireland, and is contacted by most journalists who write about this subject. He always talks about his nephew in the hope that some more publicity will shed light on what happened to him. However, in all the pieces that I have researched for both the many articles I have written and for this book, I have never read an accurate account of Aengus's disappearance. While the detail included is always correct, journalists choose to leave out other possibly important information, because they feel it would be hurtful for his family. However, if the truth is ever to come out then the full facts should be in the public domain.

Aengus was 20 years of age when he went missing on the 11 February, 2000. On the day he disappeared, he had a long drinking session with friends in the public house opposite his flat. His friends left before him, and at 11.30 he left the pub on his own to walk directly across to his flat. He never made it and has not been seen since. Aengus is 5 feet 10 inches, with blue eyes, and he walks with a slight stoop forward. When he went missing, he was wearing blue jeans and a red, white and blue Adidas jacket.

What is missing from the various reports we read about Aengus is that he had been involved in drugs and had been in trouble in Ballybunnion over drug-related activities. Aengus had crossed certain members of a drug-dealing gang in Limerick and was being sought by these people on the day of his disappearance. It is most likely that they knew he was in the pub and waited in the lane beside his flat to confront him as he made his way home. Gardaí who have investigated his disappearance in Limerick believe this to be the case, and when known gang members are brought in for questioning about other crimes in the city, they are always asked if they know what happened to Aengus Shanahan on the night he disappeared.

There are many people who believe that their missing loved ones have been murdered by gangs or criminals, but despite pleas to the Gardaí, these cases are not investigated as murders, but simply listed under missing persons.

Another youth, Stephen Finnegan, a 20-year-old from Baldoyle in Dublin, disappeared just nine days before Aengus. Despite extensive searches there has been no sighting of Stephen since. Stephen's mother searched for him, and nine days after he disappeared, she found his car in Howth, some five miles from his home. Stephen's mother is under no illusions; she does not think her son is a missing person, but the victim of a murder, and would be happier if it was investigated as such.

One person who is known to have died at the hands of a drug gang was was 17-year-old Patrick Lawlor, who went missing in Dublin in January 1999. Known to his friends as 'Whacker', he became a runner and dealer for the vicious Westies gang who are involved in the distribution of drugs in Dublin. Gardaí knew of Patrick's activities and his home was raided some months before his disappearance. When the Gardaí raided his home they seized thousands of pounds worth of heroin. Patrick was told by the Westies that he would have to pay for the seized drugs as they were in his house and he was therefore responsible for them. As he was unable to pay, Patrick was beaten and murdered by the gang who then buried his body in a grave at the ninth lock of the Grand Canal in Clondalkin.

The Westies let what had happened to Patrick be known to other dealers working for them in an effort to instil fear in them, so that they would be afraid to cross their drug bosses. However, it was these warnings that led to the discovery of Patrick's body. When another criminal was questioned after being found in possession of drugs, he told Gardaí exactly where they could find the remains of Patrick Lawlor in an effort to cut a deal for himself. When Patrick's body was found, a murder investigation was launched, however no one has yet been charged with this crime.

While Gardaí, loved ones and those with an interest in missing persons are well aware that in a lot of instances they are actually looking for bodies, they accept that it is hard for people to accept reality until the body is recovered. While there is hope, people will hang on to it and live in denial.

It is not only disputes about drugs that cause people to kill and dispose of the body in the hope that there will never be an investigation. While researching an article for the *Sunday Independent*, I was told a story by two missing persons co-ordinators in Cork, where it is believed that a young man, officially listed as missing, was in fact murdered in a dispute over land.

The co-ordinators in Cork spoke of a father in his early 40s who went missing one night after running into a public house and claiming that men who were out to get him were chasing him. The man then spent a number of hours in the basement of the pub hiding. During this time, the landlord brought him a few drinks. At closing time the man was in a very distressed state, and the publican offered to bring him to a doctor, but when the doctor smelled alcohol he refused to deal with him. The publican offered to drive him home, but a distance from the house the man asked to be let out of the car so that he could make his way home through the fields in order to avoid those who he believed would be waiting for him. He left the publican's car, entered the field heading home and was never seen again.

After his father's death, the man had signed away an interest in his rights to the family farm. He was not now happy with this decision and there appears to have been bitterness in the family.

Local people, along with members of the Missing Persons Association, carried out detailed searches of the surrounding lands, but were refused permission from the man's siblings to search the family farm of 150 acres. Those searching offered specially trained dogs that could find their brother in the event that he had fallen into a ditch while crossing the fields and lay injured, but they were told that they could not search the family holding. People involved in the search are convinced that the man was murdered because of this dispute over property, and that his body is located somewhere on the land. In reality we may never know what happened as the man is listed as a missing person and therefore no big investigation is underway.

While various groups call for a quicker response from Gardaí, saying that a specialist unit should be established, it is easy to understand why Gardaí cannot treat every case as if it were a murder or abduction. It is very difficult for Gardaí to intrude where a person may have decided to leave the home without telling his or her loved ones. This is a decision that he or she is entitled to take, and no one has any real right to interfere. The Gardaí overcome this by dividing those who have gone missing into two categories of people. The first is referred to as 'acceptable' missing persons, that is, those the Gardaí will investigate. This term 'acceptable' refers to persons under the age of 18, the elderly, the physically or mentally disabled and those whose disappearance takes place in circumstances which give rise to fears for the person's physical or moral safety. Others, referred to as 'unacceptable' are not classed as official missing persons.

In the year that Philip Cairns went missing, there were approximately 1000 other people reported missing. Ten years later, this number had increased to 1848, and in 2002 the number had increased to a staggering 2337 people. If the Gardaí were to treat all of these as a serious case, then the resources of the entire force would be tied up just on missing persons. The reality is that 99 per cent of these people return without there being any necessity for an investigation at all. Of the 1848 people that had disappeared in 1996, only eight remained missing by the year 2000. Of the 2100 that were reported missing in 2001, only nine of those were still missing by the end of 2002.

The Gardaí remain committed to making whatever resources necessary available to an investigation where they believe special circumstances exist. They also liaise with all the groups involved in the search for missing people, but of course they would like to do more.

In 2003, the Minister for Justice, Michael McDowell, announced that Irish officers would receive training from the FBI in the latest techniques and expertise available. The FBI is recognised as the most successful and best-equipped force in the world when it comes to dealing with missing persons. The Gardaí have had talks with their counterparts at the FBI centre in New York, and the missing persons bureau of the New York Police department has had several exchange programmes with their Irish colleagues.

On 14 September, 2004, the Gardaí launched a new website at www.missingkids.ie. The site will be using the latest in age progression software in an attempt to produce images of how the children who went missing in the past would look today. This development will allow more accurate images of missing persons to be circulated.

When Philip's mother Alice saw the computer image of her son as he would look today, she told one journalist: 'I'll always remember him like the way he looked in his Confirmation picture. His features were very clear in it. That is how he will remain in my mind.' The picture of Philip still sits in pride of place in the living room of the Cairns family home and Alice believes that, 'The picture has become a symbol to Irish people. I look at it in my home every single day.'

Speaking shortly after the launch of the website, Philip's mother said, 'Somebody out there knows what happened to my son and I wish they would have the courage to come forward and tell me.'

Retired Detective Inspector Gerry O'Carroll, who worked on the case of Philip Cairn's disappearance, described the haunting school photo as 'iconic'.

'He is beaming out of that photograph. Anyone would recognise the boy in the picture as Philip Cairns. It has certainly kept his memory alive. He was the first child to be the subject of a really high-profile case to disappear and the case was so bizarre that it caught the nation's attention. I still pass Philip's home every day and always think of him.'

The Gardaí who deal with the families of missing persons know better than most the suffering of those who have loved ones missing. They also know that this suffering will not end until there is closure. If this closure comes about by families being reunited, it is the perfect ending. If closure is brought about by the discovery of the remains of a loved one, we have the words of Jean Bailey, whose brother Patrick O'Driscoll went missing in 1994, when she went to see if a body that was discovered in Co. Cork was that of her brother: 'If the remains are those of Patrick, it would finally put an end to two years of torture.' Families are at least owed that.

3

Una Lynskey

On 12 October, 1971, a 19-year-old girl called Una Lynskey, from Porterstown, Ratoath in Co. Meath, met her death as she walked home at the end of a day's work. This tragedy divided a community and led to the unlawful killing of Martin Kerrigan, who was believed to be one of those responsible for her disappearance and eventual death. He was himself killed by Una's brothers and his remains dumped at the exact location where Una's body was found.

To this day, those who were found guilty of the manslaughter of Una Lynskey still protest their innocence. Equally, the Gardaí who carried out the investigation are adamant that they found the right people and justice was done, although they all believe that the sentence handed down was far too lenient.

***

Una was the fifth of 12 children of Patrick and Winifred Lynskey. Patrick moved from Belmullet to Porterstown in 1939, and he and Winifred married nine years later on 21 August, 1948. Patrick always felt like an outsider in Porterstown, even after his father gave him a farm of 28 acres. He worked his land well, and in 1962 was able to buy an adjoining farm of 66 acres for IR£5,300. Patrick said that this came as a big surprise to his neighbours, some of them even suggesting that the land commission had given him the land for nothing. Patrick recalls, 'Nobody openly objected to me buying this farm, but I felt there was a lot of petty jealousy amongst the locals.'

There were a number of incidents over the years at the Lynskey home that made Patrick feel that he was not part of the Porterstown community, but he had a deep religious faith and his first port of call to sort out problems was the parish priest. The Lynskeys were traditional farming people, who worked hard to provide for their large family.

Una Lynskey was born on 2 September, 1952, and is described by her mother as a normal, healthy child. At the age of five she went to Ratoath National School, and later transferred to the newly built Rathbeggan School, where she completed her junior education. At 13, she went to the Convent of Mercy School in Navan, where she boarded until she was 15. Una completed her Leaving Certificate examination there in 1970 and got one honour. According to her mother, Una was a hard worker and was of average intelligence.

While attending secondary school, Una did not go dancing nor did she have boyfriends. The first dance she went to, an Irish dance at the Dunshaughlin Carnival, took place a month after she completed her Leaving Certificate. Her first and only boyfriend was Patrick Kelly from Meetstown, Ashbourne in Co. Meath.

Patrick Kelly first met Una in October 1970, a few days before the wedding of his cousin PJ to Una's sister, Catherine. Una was a bridesmaid and Patrick was best man. They got on well together, and when Una was looking for a date for a school reunion dance on 20 November, 1970, she asked Patrick. This was their first date and their relationship continued for eleven months up until the time that Una was killed. Patrick had a car that allowed them go out on excursions. They went dancing, to singing pubs, and to the pictures. Una enjoyed the pictures and her mother says that she was anxious to see the film *Ryan's Daughter*, but her untimely death ensured that she never got the chance.

Una's mother, Winifred, did not mind the relationship in the beginning, but days before Una was killed, her mother told her that she did not approve of Patrick and that she did not think that they were a good match. Winifred let Patrick know how she felt, and on the last night that he was in their home, they had words. This annoyed Patrick who, as a result, told Una that he wanted to break up. This upset Una terribly.

Patrick recalls, 'Una did not want to break it off with me and she began to cry. She was still crying when we parted, and I believe she was crying when her mother called her for work that Monday morning.' He rang Una later that day and told her that it was okay, he would not be breaking it off and this cheered her up.

Una had been unwell for a number of weeks prior to her death, complaining of a pain in her side. She had told Patrick that she did not like the local doctors, and he said he would drive her to a doctor he knew in Swords, Co. Dublin. The night before Una was killed, Patrick called to her home at 8.30 pm and took her to see Dr Cox in Swords. They arrived at the doctor's surgery shortly before nine, and Patrick waited the 30 or so minutes that Una was in the surgery. Afterwards they went to the Harp bar in Swords where they had three drinks before returning home. Patrick left Una at her house at 12.45 am. This was the last time he would see her alive.

Una's sister, Sally, had told their mother that Patrick was bringing Una to a doctor because of the pains in her side. Winifred was annoyed, but decided to say nothing. When Una got up the following morning, she told her mother that she had been to Dr Cox in Swords the previous evening. Her mother asked her why she did not go to the local doctor and Una replied that she did not like him. Winifred then told Una that she thought that Patrick should not have brought her to a doctor without their permission. She said that her father would be annoyed when he heard, but she did tell Una to be sure to fill the prescription that she had been given by Dr Cox.

Una had been suffering with the pains for about two months before she died, previous to that she had always enjoyed good health. This visit to the doctor in Swords led to rumours that Una might have been pregnant when she died. However, her mother and sisters say that they know for a fact that this could not have been so.

***

In January 1971, Una had started work in the Land Commission Office on Merrion Street in Dublin. For the first seven months, Una travelled to and from work on the Dunshaughlin bus, but when her cousin Ann Gaughan got a job in Dublin, Una switched to the Ratoath bus so she could make the daily journey with her cousin. Una never expressed any fear about the evening walk she had to take from the bus stop to her home, which was just under a mile.

On Tuesday, 12 October, 1971, Una's mother Winifred rose early and prepared breakfast, which was ready when she called Una for work at 7.15 am. After breakfast, Una went to her room to say goodbye to her sister Sally before returning to the kitchen to say goodbye to her mother. She then headed off to work. This was the last time her mother would see Una alive.

That evening, Una travelled home with her cousin Ann Gaughan as usual. As well as being cousins, the two girls were close friends. They were the only two to get off the bus at the Ratoath bus stop when it arrived at approximately 6.53 pm. After they had alighted from the bus, the girls chatted for about a minute. They would normally chat longer, but this evening was the first time they had felt the cold. Ann recalls that Una was not feeling well as she had been suffering with the flu since the previous week. Una seemed to be in a hurry home. She placed her arm on Ann's and said, 'I'd better be hurrying down, I'll see you in the morning.'

On the bus, the girls had chatted about a dinner dance that they were to attend some weeks later. Una had said to Ann that she would call and arrange for the tickets for the dance when she got home. The girls were excited about the upcoming event and had arranged to go for a fitting of dresses that they were having made for the occasion

However, Ann noticed that, although Una was talking as normal, she did not appear to be her usual jolly self. She felt that Una was daydreaming, as if her mind was elsewhere. As Una walked away from the bus stop, Ann thought to herself that her cousin seemed lonely. Una had said that she hated the thought of going home, and that when she got there she would not talk to anyone. She was still upset that her mother had had words with Patrick, and had confided in Ann that she thought members of her family were not making her boyfriend welcome in her home. Una still suspected that Patrick was going to break it off with her, and she told Ann how upset she was over this. Patrick had encouraged her to move into a flat in Dublin and had indicated to Una that he was also unhappy at home, and was thinking of getting a flat himself.

As is the case with many teenagers, there was tension in Una's home because her parents did not approve of her choice of boyfriend. That night, however, when it became apparent that something was terribly wrong, all differences were put aside as family and friends went in search of Una.

***

It was after 7 pm when Una's brother, Andrew, was fixing his bike in the Lynskey yard off Porterstown Lane. As he passed the back door, his mother called him to the kitchen and said, 'Andrew, go up to Gaughan's and see if Una is there.' His brother John told him it was 7.25 pm. At this stage, Una should have been home. Andrew cycled to his cousin's house and asked if Una had called, but was informed by his uncle that she had not been there that evening. His cousin, also called John, suggested that she might have called to the house of a friend, Ann Reddon.

Meanwhile, back at the Lynskey's house, Una's father Patrick was dealing with a customer. Winifred sent for him and told him that Una was missing. The time was now 7.40 pm, and he too suggested that Una had called to Gaughan's on her way home. A few moments later, the Gaughan's arrived and said that Una had not been there. That is when the panic set in. It was unusual for Una not to come straight home, and there was nowhere for her to go on the walk home other than the Gaughan's house. Immediately Patrick, Winifred and their children began searching for Una. They headed off in the family car and checked the surrounding roads, fields and anywhere else they thought she could be. They sensed that something was terribly wrong. Word soon spread that Una was missing, and the extended family and neighbours assisted in the search for her.

Una's boyfriend Patrick had had a tiring day in work, and when he arrived home at 7.50 pm, he ate some dinner and headed to bed. He was in bed no more than five minutes when he heard a car pull up at his driveway. Patrick recalls the moment that he heard that Una was missing: 'Someone of the family called me and told me that Una was missing. I dressed and ran out, and met John Gaughan ... [Someone] asked me had I seen Una off the bus that evening ... they told me she had alighted off the bus at the top of the road at Ann Gaughan's house, and after speaking to Ann, went on her way home, but never arrived there.'

Patrick Kelly then went to the Lynskey home on Porterstown Lane and from there to Trim Garda station where he reported Una missing. When he arrived, there was no garda at the station, so

Patrick enquired in the local pub as to where he would find one. He was told to go to the back of the station, where he met the sergeant and told him that Una was missing. When he returned to the Lynskey house, Patrick joined her two brothers in their car to look for Una. His cousin took his car and looked in different areas. They all searched throughout the night. Everyone was now very concerned for Una's safety. That night, Patrick searched desperately around the roads of Ratoath, Curragh, Garristown, Ashbourne, Miltown and other localities in the area, calling back regularly to the Lynskey home in the hope that Una may have returned home or been found.

Soon the Gardaí arrived and assisted in the search for Una. Many neighbours and friends were also helping, some already fearing the worst. Superintendent PJ Keane, who was stationed at Trim Garda station, was contacted at home at 9.30 pm and told of Una's disappearance. He immediately headed for Porterstown Lane where he noticed a large crowd of people, among them two local gardaí, Sergeant Magee and Garda JF Morgan. Upon his arrival, Superintendent Keane took charge and organised the large number of people into search parties, giving each a section of Porterstown Lane and adjoining land to search.

***

At 2.30 am on the morning of 13 October, Superintendent Keane approached four men in a car on Porterstown Lane. The four men, Richard (Dick) Donnelly, Martin Kerrigan, Martin Conmey and Christopher Ennis, were in a car owned by Donnelly. They were asked if they had any information that could help in the search for Una or if they had noticed anything strange the previous evening. Donnelly, whose family had been informed earlier that evening about Una's disappearance, told Superintendent Keane that he had been driving his car along Porterstown Lane towards Fairyhouse

Road at about 7.20 pm. He said that Martin Kerrigan had been seated in the front of his car, and that they had seen another car parked on the road. They claimed that they remembered it because it had been parked in such a way that it was difficult for them to pass by. Donnelly then claimed that Kerrigan had commented that it was a Zodiac car. They remembered it was grey in colour and that the last two figures in the registration were 00. The men then pointed to the place on the road where they said the car had been parked.

Within days of Una's disappearance, there were various media reports and local stories speculating that Una had been kidnapped. Despite many additional gardaí being drafted in from neighbouring areas, the Gardaí were having no success in locating Una and concern was mounting in the area. People felt unsafe. After two days, Superintendent Keane, who was leading the investigation, said, 'We have been searching throughout the night, but can't find any sign of the girl or any clues. We have covered a radius of 20 miles. Now we are going to have to start looking for people who would have been walking down the lane around the same time as the girl.'

A few days later, members of the murder squad were asked to assist in the investigation. Statements had been taken from the occupants of most of the houses around the area, and experienced investigators were now examining these. They soon came across a number of statements that were at variance with statements already given by the young men who had spoken to Superintendent Keane on the night of Una's disappearance. The detectives decided that they wanted to have another meeting with three of the lads, Conmey, Donnelly and Kerrigan. Christopher Ennis had not been in the car with the three others earlier that evening, around the time Una had disappeared. Some gardaí had been suspicious of the three youths, who ranged in age from 19 to 23, since Una had disappeared, simply because they had been driving in the lane when Una would have been walking home.

When questioned, a number of people who had met the men later that night told Gardaí that they had not noticed the men acting strangely. No one thought that their demeanour would have indicated that they had commited, or had been involved in, a serious crime.

Donnelly had made a statement to Gardaí on 22 October. In that statement he had said that on the evening of Una's disappearance, he had collected Conmey from work at about 6.50 pm. They had driven from Loughlinstown to Kerrigan's house, which is on the road parallel to where Una lived on Porterstown Lane, just two minutes away. Kerrigan had come out of the house and chatted to them for a few minutes. His sister, Kathleen Kerrigan, had then asked if she could have a lift to a local shop so she could buy a bale of briquettes. Donnelly had driven her to the shop and left her home again. The three lads had then headed off in the car.

Donnelly continued, 'I started from Kerrigan's and drove down to the Bush, turned left on to the Navan Road and drove along to Porterstown Lane, where I turned left into the lane. The evening was fairly bright and I was driving on sidelights. I drove to Martin Conmey's and pulled up outside his house, where we chatted for about a minute. When Conmey got out, Martin Kerrigan, who had been sitting in the back seat, moved into the front passenger seat beside me.

'I continued up the lane, and above the bad bend from Conmey's I saw a car parked on its correct side facing towards me. I had to nearly stop as the car was taking up a lot of the road. I saw that this car was a Ford Zodiac mark four. It was of light grey colour ... I had a look at the number plates and there were two noughts in it ... I had to drive very slowly to get past this car and I had to go up on the bank on my left side a bit. I looked into the car and there was nobody inside the front. I didn't look in the back seat as I was watching the back of my car to see that it didn't get stuck in this other car as I passed by. I noticed that there was a briefcase of a leather type and papers on the front passenger seat. This car was completely strange to me, although I use this lane quite a lot. The nearest that I can place the time I was passing the car is twenty past seven.

'I drove on out to the Fairyhouse Road and turned left and drove along the road towards Ratoath to my own house. I reversed into the yard and left Kerrigan in the car while I went in for my dinner ... I had my dinner and it only took me about ten minutes ... Martin and I started back for to pick up Martin Conmey ... It would be about ten to eight when we picked up Martin Conmey.'

The following day, Conmey and Kerrigan had made very similar statements to investigating Gardaí. It was the content of these three statements that were at variance with statements given by other witnesses. Three people, Martin Madden, Seán Reilly and Mrs Collins, had seen Donnelly's car heading in the opposite direction to that stated by Donnelly

The statements given by Conmey, Kerrigan and Donnelly were discussed at length by the team of investigators from the Garda Technical Bureau along with local officers. It was decided that they needed to talk to the men again, and the best way to ensure that there were no errors was to bring all three men in at the same time to ask for clarification. This would prevent the men from discussing what each had said between interviews. However, the Gardaí knew that while the men were to be asked for assistance and requested to come to Trim Garda station, under no circumstances were they to be arrested. The only point that required clarification was their movement on Porterstown Lane on the evening Una disappeared.

The operation took some planning as it involved separate teams of detectives calling to the homes of the men and transporting them to the station. Superintendent Dan Murphy and Detective Sergeant Courtney arranged the operation. On the evening of

25 October, 1971, just two weeks after Una disappeared, Martin Conmey, Martin Kerrigan and Dick Donnelly were visited by both local and murder squad Gardaí.

The three young men were taken to Trim Garda station where, according to their families, a major miscarriage of justice began. The investigating officers claim that the three were not being held in custody. They were only there to attend and assist with enquiries, and according to Gardaí, could have left at any time. However, the men remained in Trim station for a period of 45 hours. All three claimed that during their time at the station, they were tortured, beaten and humiliated. They also said that they were forced to sign confessions that were dictated to them by interviewing officers.

The families of the three men were concerned by the long detention and went to Trim Garda station. As they approached, they say that they could hear the screams of Dick Donnelly, who later claimed that he had been burned with a scalding poker. Medical reports obtained some time after his release are consistent with his claims, however no one can say for definite that these were inflicted at the station.

Later, during a court hearing, Dr Clarke gave evidence that he had been visited by the men shortly after their release from Trim Garda station. Dr Clarke described Dick Donnelly's injuries to the court as follows: 'On his left arm there were four abrasions. The smallest was an inch by an inch. There was a red linear mark three inches long. There was another two inches long. There were light bruises.'

He said he was of the view that the injuries were caused by a blunt instrument, and that a fist could have caused the marks. There was also an area of bruising 14 inches long and two inches wide beneath the left shoulder blade. On the left posterior ribs there was an area of reddish bruising three inches long by one inch wide. On the right shoulder blade there was an area of bruising one inch by a half inch, and on what is called the super scapular area, there was an area of bruising one and a half inches by one inch. On both ears there was a haematoma of the earlobes. Donnelly's right jaw was swollen and tender. The injuries to the ear were visible to a layman, according to Dr Clarke, as they were a blue-black colour. When he had finished his examination of Dick Donnelly, Dr Clarke referred him to Navan Hospital.

Martin Kerrigan's father, Martin Sr., claimed that he was shocked when he visited his son. He said that Martin was curled up like a child in a corner of his cell, wearing only his underwear. Mr Kerrigan said that it was easy to observe that his son had been badly beaten. When he saw his father, Martin repeatedly told him, 'Daddy, I did nothing, I did not have anything to do with this.'

Later, Martin Kerrigan's father went to the High Court and obtained his son's immediate release, but by the time this was obtained, Martin Kerrigan had already left the station.

Had the boys suffered the beatings and intimidation that they claimed, one would have expected the families to have brought it to the attention of the Gardaí in charge of the operation as soon as the boys returned home. However, this was not the case. It was not until a bail hearing some months later that the Gardaí first heard of the allegations of intimidation and assault. When Superintendent Keane heard the details of the allegations at the bail hearing for Conmey and Donnelly, he initiated an extensive investigation, but found no evidence to substantiate the claims. Superintendent Keane also pointed out that he visited the Conmey home about another matter before the bail application, but no complaints were made to him during discussions with Martin Conmey's parents.

After many hours of interviews at Trim Garda station, Gardaí maintained that Martin Conmey felt under pressure to tell the truth. The Gardaí said that they knew from experience that he was holding back on something. Initially Conmey claimed that his statement of some days previous was correct, and when it was pointed out to him that it was at variance with what other people had said, he said they were lying. However, it was obvious that there was no reason for them to lie. They were only giving an account of which way a car was driving. The people who made the statement would have had no idea that what they were saying could possibly create trouble for the three men.

Detective Sergeant Courtney and Garda Brian Guildea say that while interviewing Conmey they chatted to him about general things, like his hobbies and his work. They were trying to gain his confidence, and it seemed to be having the desired effect. After a short break, the men returned and asked Conmey if he would tell the truth. He replied that he already had. After further requests, however, the interviewing gardaí say that Conmey raised his voice and said, 'I can't, I can't. Why has it to be me? Why can't Kerrigan and Donnelly tell it as well as me?' When it was pointed out to him that telling the truth was in his best interest, the gardaí allege that Conmey replied, 'Fair enough, I will tell you what I know.' Martin Conmey then made his statement.

What is significant about this statement is that it was made in the presence of Martin's father, David Conmey. The gardaí present recorded the comments of both father and son, and these were read out in court. Mr Conmey asked his son, 'Martin, tell the truth. I ask you now to tell all.' While Conmey was giving his statement, his mother entered the room. She listened and began to cry as he recounted what happened that night. As Conmey looked over to his mother, she said to him, 'Martin, no matter how hard it is, and it is hard, tell the truth.'

In his statement, Conmey claims that he finished work at 6.45 pm and then went in Donnelly's car to the home of Kerrigan, where they arrived at 7 pm. Kerrigan joined them in the car, and then his sister Kathleen came out and asked for a lift to the local shop. They drove her to the shop, which was just a few minutes from the house, and then brought her home again before the three men headed off in the car. At this time, Conmey was sitting in the rear seat of the car. As they were driving along Porterstown Lane, they came upon Una Lynskey who was walking to her home. As the car passed her, Conmey claims that Donnelly said to Kerrigan, 'I think I will give her a lift.' They travelled to the top of the road where Donnelly turned his car before heading back down Porterstown Lane.

As they drove back down the lane, they again came upon Una, and this time they stopped and offered her a lift home. Una walked around the front of the car as Kerrigan opened the door, and she sat in beside him on a bench-type front seat. She pulled the door closed, and then Kerrigan applied the lock. As they were approaching Una's lane, Kerrigan put his arm around her waist and she began to struggle. Una tried to open the door, but failed. As it became obvious to her that they were not letting her out of the car, she pleaded with them, asking, 'Where are you bringing me?' No one answered her. As Kerrigan put his hands around her waist again, she told him to take his hands away.

At this stage, Donnelly was driving the car faster. Una kept asking where she was being taken. As the car approached the end of Porterstown Lane, a frightened Una Lynskey again attempted to escape from the car, but as she tried to open the door handle, Kerrigan took hold of her hand and prevented her.

Conmey then states that Kerrigan tried to put his hands around Una's waist again, and that she made a little movement in an attempt to avoid his roving hands. Suddenly Donnelly stopped the car, and as he did, Una fell sideways and hit her head against the glass on the passenger door. At this stage, Conmey observed that Una appeared to become weak. Then, according to Conmey's statement, Donnelly turned left toward Dublin.

'He [Donnelly] stopped his car and asked me was I getting out. I said, "I will," and I got out the left rear door. Una's head was still on the glass, but she was not as beat looking. As we were parting, Donnelly said, "I will see you." He then drove off towards Dublin. I watched his car until he travelled for about three hundred yards and in that distance he did not stop or turn off the main road – I walked home by Porterstown Lane and I arrived home at about 7.25 pm.'

Martin Conmey added that as he got out of the car, Una Lynskey looked back at him but said nothing. According to Conmey, he rejoined Donnelly and Kerrigan, along with some others, later that night as they went to various pubs for an evening's entertainment. People who observed the men that night agree that they did not look like lads who had just committed a serious offence. It was while returning home from their night out that they met Superintendent Keane.

This statement was seen as a major breakthrough in the investigation and led to new enquiries being made by investigating officers. It also resulted in further interviews with all three men who were at the station assisting with Garda enquiries. Conmey's statement was not, however, the only admission allegedly made in Trim that night.

Martin Kerrigan was also being interviewed by a team of detectives, and when he was made aware of Conmey's confession, he obviously felt the game was up. How this was achieved is best explained by one of the investigating garda who was involved in the interviews that night.

'The night that Conmey confessed, I was in the Superintendent's office when Martin Kerrigan was brought into the office. Detective Sergeant Courtney was also present. I heard Martin Conmey ask Kerrigan if he remembered the evening they were searching the fields for Una, and Kerrigan replied that he did remember. Conmey then said to Kerrigan, "Do you remember Donnelly telling us that he put her under a bridge near Lucan and he told us not to say anything about it?" Conmey said to Kerrigan something to the effect, "Martin, you must remember that."'

According to the garda, Kerrigan then admitted that he remembered Donnelly saying it. But as he continued, Kerrigan said that he and Donnelly had taken Una to Clonee and then out on the Lucan Road to a bridge near Lucan, where they had stopped the car. Kerrigan said, 'I took the body out of the car and I put it in some bushes near the bridge. Donnelly got out and stood beside the car, but he didn't help me to shift the body.' Although Kerrigan's statement is contradictory, this did not come out in court as Martin Kerrigan was killed before any trials took place, and therefore his statement was not introduced.

What is most strange is that none of the men were ever asked how Una died, and this information was never offered in their statements.

After Kerrigan made his admission, Donnelly was brought in to him. Donnelly, however, maintained his position that he knew nothing of the events that occurred that night. He still claimed that he had not given Una a lift, and that she had not been in his car on the evening she disappeared. While in custody, Conmey and Kerrigan signed confessions, but Donnelly refused.

When Martin Conmey had made his confession, Mr and Mrs Lynskey, along with the parish priest, Fr Cogan, arrived at Trim Garda station. When Mrs Lynskey was asked in court who it was that suggested she go to the Garda station, she said that when she had heard from her daughter that a number of men had been brought to Trim Garda station in relation to Una's disappearance, she had discussed the matter with her husband. She said it was he who had suggested they go and talk to Martin Conmey as they both knew him well. Una's parents believed that if Conmey had any information, he would help them. At 1.30 pm, Mr Lynskey went to the parish priest, Fr Cogan, and asked if he would accompany them to the station. In an unusual and unprecedented development, Conmey, a man who had now admitted to being involved in Una's abduction, was allowed time alone with her mother, father and the local parish priest. In a statement given to police, Una's mother recalls what was a horrific experience for her.

'On Tuesday, 26 October, 1971, I was in Trim Garda station. At about 5 pm I spoke with Martin Conmey [who] was in a room there. I know him well and he knows me well. We are next-door neighbours. I was alone with him, and the reason I was alone with him was that a few minutes previously, my husband, Patrick Lynskey, and Fr Cogan, PP Ratoath, also spoke to Martin Conmey.'

Fr Cogan became very upset. He started to cry and as he was comforted by Mrs Lynskey he appealed to Conmey to tell them what he knew, 'Martin, if only it were to administer the last rites to her [Una], … you know, Martin, we'll all have to appear before our creator one day.'

In her statement, Mrs Lynskey continues, 'My husband and I asked Martin Conmey did he know where my daughter Una was, or could he help me in any way to find her, dead or alive. I begged him to tell me. I said to him, "Suppose your sister Mary was missing, how would your mother feel?" He nodded, "I know. Could I see you, Mrs Lynskey, on your own?" I said, "Yes," and then Fr Cogan and my husband left the room and closed the door. [As soon as] they left, Martin commenced to tell me.'

Conmey told Mrs Lynskey that he had been in Donnelly's car with Kerrigan and Donnelly, and that they had come across Una on the road. Una's mother could not believe that Una had taken a lift from them, as she knew that Una did not like Donnelly and his gang. Conmey explained that Una had tried to get out of the car, but that Kerrigan would not allow her. Mrs Lynskey then asked him where Una was and if she was still alive. Conmey replied that yes, Una was alive, and he thought she was somewhere in Dublin, maybe a flat in Ballymun. When asked where in Ballymun, he replied, 'I can't tell, I can't tell.' He would later claim that he told Mrs Lynskey this because he could not think of anything else to say to her.

When Conmey was questioned in court about his statement, he said it was all lies. He was asked why he claimed that he had made his statement under duress when his mother and father, who were present, saw no indication that he was being mistreated or that he was under pressure. The gardaí had simply asked him to tell the truth. The court enquired as to how he could then claim he was under pressure. Conmey replied that his father had been very rough towards him and did not believe that he was innocent. He said that his mother had not been as bad. Conmey told the court, 'I don't know, My Lord. I felt my father and mother were gone against me. I felt nobody believed me, and I felt I had to go along and say what the guards wanted me to say. My mind was gone that far, going without sleep.'

However, it was when the three men left Trim Garda station that the real trouble began for them. Shots were fired over their houses, insults, such as 'murdering bastards', were painted on the roads outside their homes. Despite the fact that the body of Una Lynskey had not yet been located, her family and relatives were convinced that Conmey, Kerrigan and Donnelly were responsible for her death. Tensions in the area ran high; there were constant scuffles between members of the extended families on both sides, which became more violent as time went on.

No matter how much the three young men pleaded their innocence, their claims seemed to fall on deaf ears. Local people who had made statements to Gardaí that tied in with statements made by the three men regarding their movements on the evening that Una disappeared, seem to have been ignored by investigating Gardaí. The Lynskey family was told by a member of the Gardaí that the three had admitted to the crime. At one stage, a member of the investigating team suggested to the Lynskey family that they say a rosary as Gardaí were going down to the river. The family were told that one of the three men who were brought into Trim station claimed they had dumped Una's body there.

***

Six weeks after the confessions were made at Trim Garda station, on 10 December, 1971, the body of Una Lynskey was found. James Williams, a farmer who worked with Dublin County Council, was carrying out work at Glendhu at Enniskerry, Co. Wicklow. He recalls that on that day, he and his colleague were cleaning out a drain on the left-hand side of the road at Glendu. Williams crossed over the road and walked alongside a wire fence, which was surrounding a forest area. His attention was drawn to a pile of fir bushes that were lying behind a clump of rhododendrons. Williams was aware that there were no fir bushes in that particular area, and decided to climb the fence and have a closer look. He thought that maybe a dead sheep had been buried there. There were more bushes dumped than he originally thought, so he got a shovel to remove them. As he removed the last of the bushes, he noticed some rotten felt which was being held down by an old grate. Williams removed the grate, and as he unfolded the felt, he realised that it had been used to conceal a body. He saw a human skull. Williams immediately told his colleague what he had discovered, and they returned home where they called the Gardaí.

At 11.40 am, Sergeant Gallagher received the call for which the Gardaí had been waiting. James Williams informed him that he had found what appeared to be human remains. Gallagher told Williams to stay at the scene and not to touch anything. When he arrived, Sergeant Gallagher was in no doubt that it was a human body, and that the remains had been there for some time. He could see a human skull and also a ribcage without flesh or tissue. The rest of the body was covered by a dark felt, and it appeared that no grave had been dug. The body had been dumped in a hurry, with the feet facing the road.

The Gardaí then contacted the State Pathologist, Professor Maurice Hickey, and requested that he attend Rathfarnham Garda station so that Superintendent Flynn could bring him to the scene to examine the body. The remains were then removed to University College Dublin, where a detailed examination was carried out.

Professor Hickey noted: 'The remains consisted of a human skeleton with a small amount of human flesh remaining in places. As a result of decomposition, no portion of the brain and no internal organs of the chest or abdomen were present.' This in itself made it impossible to determine the cause of death. However, he added, 'I examined the skull, the bones of the spine, the ribs, pelvis and both arms and legs. There were no fractures of any of these bones.'

While the cause of death could not be established, the state of decomposition was consistent with a body that had been dead for a period of two or three months. Professor Hickey removed a wristwatch and gold ring from the body, which were passed to Gardaí as evidence. On 15 December, 1971, Sergeant Magee from Dunshaughlin showed these items to Una's boyfriend who identified them as gifts he had given to Una during their relationship. The fact that there were no fractures to any of the bones ruled out any chance that Una had been involved in a motor accident. The findings made it possible that Conmey had told the truth, that she just fell, yet remained conscious while he was in the car.

Now that Una's body had been found, tensions ran even higher, and the atmosphere in the area was one of anger. It was obvious to all that something serious was about to happen. Such was the concern that a local garda had been asked by his superiors to look out for the safety of the three men who had been questioned and who were alleged to have made confessions. It would be a number of days before Gardaí would be ready to arrest the men and question them further, as they were awaiting the results of the post mortem, as well as details of other evidence or clues found at the area where Una's body was found.

Just as a community was coming to terms with the tragic death of Una Lynskey, a vicious act of revenge took place.

***

On 19 December, 1971, Martin Kerrigan, one of the three men arrested and questioned about Una's disappearance, was abducted and savagely murdered. Kerrigan was the one who, according to Conmey, had prevented Una from leaving the car, and who had put his hands around her waist.

On that Sunday afternoon, Kerrigan went drinking with some friends in Ratoath. They drank from 4 o'clock in the afternoon until pub closing time, and were hanging around the street before going to a dance. Kerrigan and his friends were all fairly intoxicated at this stage.

Around this time, Garda Harty of Ashbourne arrived in Ratoath, and saw Kerrigan and his friends hanging around. Garda Harty noticed that Una Lynskey's boyfriend, Patrick Kelly, was in a car down the street with a group of men. In order to avoid a row, Garda Harty offered Kerrigan and his friends a lift to the dance and they accepted.

While Garda Harty was driving the men to the dance, however, he came upon the scene of an accident. He left the car and took the two drivers into a house to sort out the details of the accident. The young men, including Kerrigan, then got out of Garda Harty's car. A few minutes later, two cars arrived at the scene, one driven by Una Lynskey's cousin, John Gaughan, and the other by her boyfriend, Patrick Kelly. Two of Una's brothers, John and James, were in Gaughan's car.

The two Lynskey brothers and John Gaughan got out of their car and headed towards Kerrigan and his friends, who were standing at the crossroads. There was an exchange of words and a long and vicious fight broke out between the two rival groups. During the row, Kerrigan was pushed to the ground. He was then grabbed by one of the Lynskey brothers and dragged to Gaughan's car. He was bundled into the back seat where the two Lynskey brothers sat on him and held him down. When Garda Harty returned to his car, he became aware of what had happened. He noticed that Martin Kerrigan was gone and that tensions at the scene were running dangerously high. The row between the opposing groups was still ongoing so Garda Harty summoned reinforcements to help him restore order and break up the fighting.

John Gaughan drove the car containing Martin Kerrigan and the Lynskey brothers to the spot in the mountains where Una Lynskey's body had been found. As he drove, John and James Lynskey continually beat Kerrigan's head off the bar on the back of the front seat. They also pulled his hair and punched him constantly. On the way, they stopped for petrol, and in order to quieten Kerrigan, they covered his mouth. After this he showed no sign of life. The three kidnappers claim that they did not realise that Kerrigan was unconscious and told him, 'We're coming near to the spot now.'

Meanwhile, the original fight had moved to the home of the Gaughan's, as friends of Kerrigan became concerned about his well-being. Garda reinforcements had arrived and at this stage there were about twenty Gardaí trying to control a very angry crowd.

At 1.15 am, Gaughan and the two Lynskey brothers returned to Gaughan's home. Superintendent Moore, who was in charge, questioned Gaughan, who admitted that they had taken Kerrigan away in the car and dumped him in the mountains. Gaughan told the superintendent that earlier that day, Kerrigan had jeered Una Lynskey's mother as she visited her daughter's grave. Garda Harty then spoke to Gaughan and John Lynskey, and they told him that they had taken Kerrigan to the spot where Una's body had been found. They admitted roughing him up, but said they did not think he was dead. They conceded that he had not been moving, but claimed they thought he was playacting. By this time, the crowd had grown outside the Gaughan house, and Superintendent Moore suggested that they go to the police station to finish the interview.

By now, Gardaí in Dublin had been alerted that Martin Kerrigan had been left close to where the body of Una had been found. At 3 am on 20 December, the Gardaí recovered his body. John Gaughan and the Lynskey brothers were immediately informed that Martin Kerrigan was dead. John Gaughan replied, 'Jesus Christ almighty, we will have to face up to it,' while John Lynskey said, 'I don't care if I am strung up in the morning.' His brother James made no reply. The three claimed that while they had Kerrigan in the car, he admitted that he and the others were responsible for killing Una.

Martin Kerrigan had been brutally mutilated and beaten where he lay. The State Pathologist, Professor Maurice Hickey, who examined the body the day it was found, said the front of the chest and the abdomen were exposed, and the trousers had been ripped down to the knees along the seams. Both eyes and the nose and mouth were badly bruised as were the head, back, shoulders and arms. The worst injury was a cut with a jagged edge, three inches along the left side of the groin, extending through the skin. This injury, which was in effect castration, was inflicted after death. The pathologist estimated the time of death to have been between midnight and 2 am on the morning of 20 December, 1971.

One former sergeant said about Kerrigan's abduction: 'When the three men [Donnelly, Conmey and Kerrigan] were released, it was well known locally that they had made certain admissions while detained in Trim Garda station, hence the reason why

Martin Kerrigan was abducted and murdered. This was something that should not have happened.'

John Gaughan and John and James Lynskey were subsequently charged with murder. In March 1972, they were found guilty of manslaughter and received a two-year sentence. At the trial, prosecuting counsel told the jury that there had been a two-fold motive in the case. The first, to extract a confession from Kerrigan, and the second, to seek revenge for the death of Una Lynskey.

***

Soon after Una's body was discovered, the Gardaí arrested both Martin Conmey and Dick Donnelly, and charged them with the murder of Una Lynskey. Their trial opened at the end of June 1972 and lasted thirteen days.

The trial was full of allegations about police brutality, but the only evidence offered to support this was the medical report given to the court by Dr Clarke about the injuries to Dick Donnelly. These allegations were strongly denied by all the Gardaí involved. There had been an internal Garda inquiry carried out before the trial, and it had concluded that there was no substance to the allegations made by the accused men. Therefore, claims of brutality did not stand up in court, and the jury accepted the case that was presented by the prosecution.

As well as the confessions made in Trim Garda station, the prosecution also had another witness who swore that Martin Conmey had confessed to his part in Una's disappearance before her remains had been found. This witness was Conmey's flatmate, Thomas Mangan from Belmullet. Mangan was employed as a labourer, and worked on a site with Conmey in March 1971. Mangan told the court that he knew Conmey from work and that one day Conmey had asked him where he could get lodgings. The two men moved in together and one evening, while they were in the flat, Conmey told Mangan, 'I killed her.' Mangan told the court that Conmey had told him that Donnelly's car had hit Una and knocked her unconscious as she walked along the road. He and Donnelly had then put Una into the back of the car, and moved her to a ditch beside a mountain where they hid her body. According to Mangan, Conmey had told him this before Una's body was found.

In his charge to the jury, the judge outlined the difficulties surrounding this case. He explained the law, and how they should consider the evidence that they had heard. After many hours' deliberation, and having come back and clarified matters with the judge, the jury found the two accused not guilty of murder, but guilty of manslaughter. They found that Una had been killed while in the car, but that this had not been intentional, and it was more likely boisterous behaviour that had gone too far.

In passing sentence, the judge said, 'This is a case with tragic connotations ... a young girl, Una Lynskey, disappeared suddenly and her body was found a long time afterwards. The jury, after very full consideration of the facts of this case, found the two accused guilty of manslaughter rather than murder. I have to give respect to their judgement. The less I say about the facts of the case the better, because it has emerged that two young people have lost their lives. Martin Kerrigan, who is said to have been involved with the two men before me today in the death of Una Lynskey, was killed in circumstances which led to a verdict of manslaughter in which three people were sentenced, and out of these two deaths a number of lives have been blighted. In all the circumstances, I am unable to define between the guilt of the two accused, but giving the fullest weight to what has been so forcibly said on their behalf by their respective counsel, I consider that I am giving effect to their previous good record, to the words of commendation that have been spoken on their behalf by their parents, by the parish priest, and also what has been urged by counsel. I sentence each to three years penal servitude.'

On 15 July, 1972, Martin Conmey and Dick Donnelly were sentenced to three years in prison, but both men obtained bail on 31 July, pending the outcome of their appeals.

Donnelly succeeded in his appeal against his conviction, while Conmey's conviction was upheld and he served his full sentence. The success of Donnelly's appeal was largely based on the fact that he did not sign a confession admitting to having participated in any way in this crime.

***

The unlawful killing of Una Lynskey was not an intentional act. All those involved in investigating this case firmly believe that Una's death was a freak accident. It would appear that when Una had the accident, those responsible for keeping her in the car panicked. However, whatever the cause of her death, those of us who have not suffered a similar experience cannot really understand the pain and suffering endured by Una's family. Nor indeed can we feel the pain of the family of Martin Kerrigan, a young man so brutally killed and mutilated. This double tragedy has caused a great deal of unnecessary suffering in this small rural community.

4

Richie Barron

Had circumstances been different and had Richard (Richie) Barron gone to visit his daughter Geraldine on 13 October, 1996, he might still be alive today. Richie's wife, Nora, and other members of his family had gone to visit Geraldine in hospital in Derry, as she had given birth to her first child the previous day. Richard had decided to leave the visit until a later occasion. Instead he went to Raphoe town in Co. Donegal to celebrate the good news of his grandson's birth.

Richie Barron had just turned 54 and lived at The Commons, Raphoe. He was a man of modest means with a small holding of 1.5 acres and made his living dealing cattle and horses. Richard was well known to most people in Raphoe and was regarded as a real character. He was known to like a drink, and when under the influence could be extremely loud and sometimes verbally abusive. However, most people took no offence as they also knew that Richie was a kind man who was known for his generosity. It would be accurate to say that he was popular with most townsfolk.

On 13 October, Richie left his house at 5.45 pm for what would be the last time and started out on a 45-minute walk into Raphoe town. During the next six hours, Richie went on a pub-crawl, visiting a number of public houses and consuming a considerable amount of alcohol during the course of the evening. His first port of call was the Central Hotel, where he enjoyed his first few drinks of the evening, and he stayed there until 9.30 pm. His next stop was the Town and Country public house, where he consumed more drink and stayed until 11.30 pm. Like many a person on a night out, Richie was spending more money than he had anticipated and left this pub on one occasion to go to the Tir Chonaill bar where he cashed a cheque.

By 11 pm Richie Barron had consumed a lot of alcohol and he became involved in an argument with a local man, Mark McConnell in the Town and Country pub. Richie had been staring at young McConnell throughout the evening, and at one stage, when McConnell was returning from the gents, Richie tugged at his jacket. An argument developed during which Richie told McConnell that he was 'a poor excuse for a McBrearty', McConnell being related to the McBreartys. The McBreartys were a successful family who had returned many years before from Scotland and built up successful businesses in Raphoe. They owned a nightclub and a public house. There had been bad blood between the McBreartys and the Barrons for nearly twenty years, ever since a fight between Frank McBrearty Jr. and Richie Barron's son, Stephen, in which young McBrearty came out the better of the two. The fight had taken place in the centre of Raphoe, in an area known as the Diamond and had been witnessed by many. It was the talk of the area for years and is still referred to by many locals as the cause of the problems between the two families.

When Richie made the remark, a fight broke out and the proprietor of the bar, Mark Quinn, moved in and separated the two men. McConnell was brought to another room, and soon after, Richie left the bar. That was the end of this confrontation.

Richie then headed for another pub, the Suile Tavern. He arrived there at 11.45 pm. When he arrived he was noticeably drunk, but according to the barman who let him in that night, 'Richie was drunk, but not legless.' Richie ordered a small whiskey and joined his friend Phonsie Crawford at the bar. While he was drinking at the Suile Tavern, he had his second argument that we are aware of that night. This time the row was with Manny

Heggarty, and with Manny it was a more serious confrontation. Richie was sitting at the bar, and Manny was shouting at him. Manny was insisting that he was owed money by Richie from a horse deal between the two men that had gone wrong. Soon the argument developed into a scuffle and the men had to be separated.

Richie Barron was going to leave the pub after the argument, but his friend Phonsie told him to stay and finish his drink. He eventually left at about 12.30 am. A barman showed him to the door and offered to get him a taxi. Richie declined the offer, saying he would walk home. His spirits were high and he joked that his trousers were falling because his button kept opening.

As he made his way home, Richie was seen by a number of people who were also out socialising that night. By the time he left the Suile Tavern, witnesses say he was extremely drunk and was negotiating his way home by holding onto the walls with both hands. One girl, Roberta Browne, saw him at about 12.35 am. As she walked by him he caught her by her jacket and asked her if she was okay for money or if she wanted a few pounds. She said, 'No thanks,' and continued on her way. She realised Richie had consumed a lot of drink, and when she looked back he was gone, obviously heading out on the road home.

***

Richie Barron was killed as he headed home some time between 12.45 and 12.55 am on the morning of 14 October, 1996. Local man Lee Parker was the person who first discovered Richie's body. This was not the first time that Lee had seen Richie had that night. He had seen him some minutes earlier when Richie had left the Suile Tavern public house.

As Lee approached the Glenmaquinn Road, at Townparks, Raphoe, in his car, he noticed a man lying on the road. In his statement to police Lee Parker recalls, 'I saw a man lying on the road ... I had a fair idea it was Richie Barron, because I saw him drunk down town earlier. I pulled out to go around him and saw blood on the road. Just beyond the body, I turned the car and drove back by the body again. As I was driving slowly past him, I saw it was definitely Richie Barron ... He was lying on his back, parallel with the hedge ... his legs were crossed from the knees down only. I saw a big hole in his forehead. The blood was running down the top of his head and going towards the hedge ... I saw no other marks on him ... I saw a serious amount of thick blood around his head on the road ... all I saw was Richie and the blood ... I didn't get out of the car at all. I drove on a few yards to McBride's gate and parked. I ran in and knocked on the door. I told Rita to phone the guards or an ambulance ... I looked at my watch and saw it was 12.55 am.'

After raising the alarm, Lee returned to the body, and noticed that a number of people had arrived at the scene. One of those was Seán Duffy, who tried to find a pulse. Richie Barron was pronounced dead an hour later, but prior to the hospital advising the Gardaí of this, no one was sure of his condition. Seán also noticed a scrape on Richie's forehead and observed a large amount of blood where he lay.

A few minutes later, Richie's son Stephen, who had been contacted at home by a person who had come upon the scene, arrived and tended to his father. He tried to help his father get some air and attempted to comfort him while they awaited the arrival of the ambulance.

Garda Patrick Boyce was on duty at the communications centre at Letterkenny Garda station when the call concerning Richie Barron came through. It was 1.05 am when he received a call from Hilary McBride advising him that Richie Barron had been struck by a car and was lying on the side of the road. She told him that she had already phoned for an ambulance before contacting the Gardaí.

Garda Boyce tried to contact Garda Patrick Mulligan by radio, as Garda Mulligan was on duty in Raphoe. However, he failed to get a response. In an attempt to get Gardaí to the scene as quickly as possible, Garda Boyce then contacted Lifford Garda station and passed the details on to Garda PJ McDermott.

It was 1.20 am when the ambulance arrived at the scene. As soon as the drivers attended Richie, they knew his injuries were serious. The ambulance men noticed a lot of blood running from Richie's head. One of the ambulance men, Mr Monaghan, contacted his base and reported that it appeared to have been a hit-and-run accident. He suggested the Gardaí should be contacted straight away. While the second ambulance man was treating Richie, he noticed that Richie was bleeding from the nose and mouth. However, he did not observe any evidence of a motor accident, he could see no broken glass, no skid marks, none of the usual tell-tale signs that he would normally observe.

By the time Richie Barron was taken from the scene by the ambulance, the Gardaí had still not arrived. This long delay was unusual, and subsequently led to a lot of speculation about what the local Gardaí were doing that night at the time Richie was attacked.

Richie Barron was admitted to Letterkenny Hospital at 1.50 am on 14 October, 1996. Following examination and efforts to revive him, he was pronounced dead.

***

When Gardaí at the communications centre in Letterkenny were unable to contact Garda Mulligan at Raphoe, two gardaí from nearby Lifford station were sent to the scene at Townparks. These were Garda John Birney and Garda James McDwyer. At first the two guards headed for Raphoe Garda station because they needed directions to the scene of the accident. When they arrived at the station, they were surprised to find it empty, they thought that someone would be in or about the station. They then headed to an area known as Townparks, which was on the right just past the Garda station, but they saw no sign of an accident there. They were aware that there were a few 'Townparks' in Raphoe, and decided to head towards the Diamond in the centre of Raphoe in the hope of discovering where the accident had taken place.

As the patrol car approached the Diamond, they saw Garda Mulligan in conversation with a local man who they recognised as Steven McCullagh. They noticed that Garda John O'Dowd from Raphoe station, who was off duty, was also there in his own car. Garda McDwyer asked Mulligan if he was aware of the accident and Mulligan told him that he was just being given the details by McCullagh. While they waited for Garda Mulligan to finish speaking with McCullagh, the two Lifford gardaí spoke to Garda O'Dowd.

When Garda Mulligan was finished, he joined O'Dowd in his car and asked the gardaí in the patrol car to follow them to the scene of the accident. The four gardaí arrived at the scene at 1.35 am, and on arrival noticed that a large crowd had gathered at the roadway. The gardaí then carried out an examination of the scene.

Garda McDwyer from Lifford walked up and down the road and found a piece of human flesh with hair attached. He lifted it up to examine it and then placed it back on the road, rather than keeping it for evidence. In his statement, Garda McDwyer says, 'I examined the scene closely again and, curiously, nothing was present to indicate a vehicle, no dirt marks, no impact area, no paint flakes or glass. I walked the area, studying the road closely. I found a piece of human skin with hair attached to it lying on the road adjacent to a pool of blood ... I could find no other foreign object at the scene.'

When they finished examining the scene, Garda McDwyer approached the people present and asked if any of them had witnessed an accident. Lee Parker came forward and told him that he had discovered the body and asked Rita McBride, in the house nearby, to call an ambulance. Seán Duffy explained that he too had come across the body of Richie Barron, and tried without success to locate a pulse. He said that the body had been extremely cold.

From his discussions and from what he observed at the scene, Garda McDwyer formed the view that Richie Barron had been the victim of a hit-and-run accident. While still at the scene, the Gardaí were advised that Richie Barron had been pronounced dead at Letterkenny General Hospital.

At this stage, all four gardaí left the scene without taking any steps to close it off, even though they now knew that a man had died there and that someone was responsible for his death. If it had been a hit-and-run, they were now investigating a case of manslaughter at the very least, and the possibility that it was murder was also present. It is strange then that the Gardaí took no steps to preserve the scene. Instead, Garda O'Dowd headed off to check on a person he knew who drove a car without insurance, while the other three gardaí went to Letterkenny General Hospital to take possession of Richie Barron's clothes for examination. When they arrived, they were told that the family of Richie Barron were there with the body, so arrangements were made for his personal effects to be collected at a later stage.

The behaviour of the four gardaí that night is strange to say the least. The Gardaí knew Richie Barron. Some of them were also aware of a rumour that Richie had been having an affair with the wife of a serving garda in the Donegal region. It is believed by some in Raphoe that there is more to be learned about Garda involvement in the death of Richie Barron. Many believe that certain gardaí are well aware of exactly what happened to Richie that night, but didn't want the real story behind his death to emerge. A number of people in the Raphoe area believe the subsequent investigation was designed to direct investigators away from the real perpetrators of this crime. While none of these allegations suggest that anyone set out to murder Richie Barron, many believe that it could have been a beating that went wrong. There are other stories that suggest that a member of the Gardaí knocked Richie down, and another that Richie was staggering in the middle of the road when two gardaí who were trying to pass in their car roared at him to make way. It was suggested that Richie became abusive, and one of the gardaí got out of the car and assaulted him, when they realised how hard they had hit him, and saw that he may have fatal injuries, they then brought his body out onto the road and placed it in such a way as to make it appear that a car had hit him.

Whatever about Gardaí involvement in Richie Barron's death that night, according to experienced investigators the inaction of the four gardaí who attended the scene is unprecedented. Their failure to observe the most basic steps prompted the following comments from one of their superiors, Superintendent John Fitzgerald: 'I received a telephone call at 7.45 that morning from Garda John McManus, Garda Communications Room, Letterkenny. I was notified by him that a fatal hit-and-run accident had occurred at Raphoe at about 1 am ... I immediately made enquiries from Garda McManus as follows. Was the scene properly preserved? Who was the Scenes of Crime Examiner? Was there proper identification and was that end of things covered? Was the injured party's clothing taken possession of? Was anybody [arrested] or were there suspects? ... Why was I not immediately notified? ... I rang Garda McManus and expressed my total dismay at not being notified, because during my time as Superintendent at Letterkenny for nearly five years, all the points raised were emphasised over and over again and were always covered.'

On hearing that four gardaí attended the scene, and that it was not yet preserved and had not been examined by a Scenes of Crime Examiner, Superintendent Fitzgerald said, 'I was very annoyed, disappointed and surprised by the initial actions of the four gardaí, who are all experienced and well used to serious incidents.' These comments, made by a senior officer in Donegal, fuelled the rumours that in some way the Gardaí were involved in a cover-up rather than an investigation.

***

The standard of investigative work carried out by the gardaí that night was to become a regular feature in the investigation into the death of Richie Barron. It was to become one of the biggest embarrassments for An Garda Síochána since its foundation.

Even though orders were given by Superintendent Fitzgerald at 8.30 am the following day that an officer immediately attend the scene, a full hour elapsed before the scene was in fact attended and sealed off by Gardaí. This long and unexplained delay may have resulted in evidence, essential if the crime was to be solved, being washed away. Such evidence could never be recovered.

The road where Richie's body was discovered was used by many children on their way to the local school. Two local men, Derek Connolly and Simon McBride, were disturbed at the amount of blood that remained on the roadside. They felt that this should not be witnessed by the young children. As the scene had not been sealed off by the Gardaí, the men assumed that they had already finished their investigation and they had removed any important evidence that may have existed. This being the case, the men decided to wash the blood away, at the same time destroying vital evidence. They were not to know this, however, and were only doing what they believed was right.

When the Gardaí eventually arrived to secure the scene, they found the two men washing away the evidence with a yard brush. Simon McBride examined the ground carefully before he did this, and is satisfied that there was no broken glass or other debris that would indicate that there had been a car accident.

***

At this stage most people still believed that Richie Barron had died as a result of a hit-and-run accident. However, within the next few hours things were to change. Detective Sergeant JS Henry went to the morgue and carried out a visual examination of the body, during which he noticed a number of wounds on the hands of Richie Barron.

In a subsequent statement regarding this issue, Sergeant Henry said: 'I was suspicious as to the cause of death and left the hospital to report to my superiors. I spoke to Inspector Gallagher at the Garda station and accompanied him back to the morgue to review the body ... I did not touch the body on the second visit, but remained there while Inspector Gallagher had a look at the body. We left a short time later. I am unable to say whether the marks on the backs of the hands or the injuries to his fingers were defence marks. I felt it suspicious that he had these marks on his hands, yet no other marks or injury to any other part of his body other than his head.'

What has caused concern at subsequent inquiries is the fact that a member or members of the Gardaí suspected foul play and yet this vital information was not passed to the local pathologist, Dr Barry.

It is vital to advise a local pathologist of any such concerns before he or she carries out a post-mortem. This is done as a matter of course, because where there is any suspicion of foul play, the State Pathologist, rather than the local pathologist, should be asked to carry out a post mortem. Dr Barry says that had the Gardaí made him aware of their suspicions, he would have declined to do the autopsy. The Gardaí also failed to inform Dr Barry that there had been a piece of flesh with hair attached to it found at the scene. This information is crucial because such flesh is often found where there has been an accident involving a motor vehicle, and by failing to supply the full detail of what they knew to Dr Barry, the Gardaí restricted him in his task.

Dr Barry carried out the autopsy at 3.30 pm on the afternoon of 14 October, 1996. In his report he details a number of injuries that he observed on the body: 'A Y-shaped laceration with crushed edges ... was found extending into mid line of the forehead to behind the hairline ... Fractured skull bone visible beneath. Bleeding from left ear. Dermal bruising on both sides of gaping wound in forehead. Abrasions on left side of this wound ... Scattered abrasions back of right hand and wrist and right index finger. Abrasions knuckle of left hand. Little left finger showed laceration of tip region.'

When Dr Barry completed the autopsy, he suspected that Richie Barron had been murdered and he made the Gardaí aware of this. He concluded that the findings would be unusual for a road traffic accident, and that it was more likely that death had been caused by a blow from a blunt instrument.

The cause of Richie Barron's death may never be discovered, but it is reasonable to assume that if a forensic pathologist had examined his remains before his burial, the truth may have emerged.

Richie Barron was buried after 10 o'clock requiem mass on 16 October, 1996, but it would appear that even that morning Superintendent John Fitzgerald had some concerns and was anxious to clarify matters before allowing the burial to go ahead. Fitzgerald consulted with Dr Barry and arranged to fax the pathologist's report to the State Pathologist Professor Harbison, which both pathologists then discussed on the phone. Professor Harbison enquired if photographs had been taken at the post mortem, and he was told that photographs of the post mortem had been taken by a garda. Professor Harbison told Superintendent Fitzgerald that Dr Barry's pathologist report was very detailed and that it would be duplication for him to examine the body of Richard Barron. His considered opinion was that the burial should go ahead. Superintendent Fitzgerald then contacted the coroner advising him of the position and he then directed burial.

However, when Professor Harbison actually saw the photographs taken during the post mortem, he said that the quality left a lot to be desired. In fact, he claimed they were practically useless because they did not show the full body of the deceased washed down and naked. Professor Harbison also pointed out that the crucial second head injury had not been photographed. The question of the hand injuries, which had led Sergeant Henry to suspect foul play and therefore bring a superior officer back to the morgue, were not properly photographed in the picture album supplied to Professor Harbison.

Harbison stated: 'Since neither the pathologist nor his attendant appeared to have cleaned the dead man's hand prior to photography, the hand pictures are worthless.' In a letter to Assistant Commissioner with responsibility for the Northern Region, Kevin Carty, in March 2000, Professor Harbison said that he would be willing to examine the body should it be exhumed.

On 12 February, 1999, the Carty inquiry was established after Kevin Carty conveyed his apprehension about the suspected involvement of a Garda in a failed extortion attempt in Raphoe in 1996. The conduct of the Garda investigation of that crime was also to be brought into question. Chief Superintendent Austin McNally and a team of investigators were appointed to carry out the special inquiry under the direction of the Kevin Carty. They were to investigate all matters concerning the Garda investigation into the death of Richie Barron. This was later expanded to cover a much wider brief, following allegations against Gardaí of corruption in the Donegal region by the estranged wife of a serving member of the force. Mrs Sheenagh McMahon, estranged wife of detective Garda Noel McMahon, had reported that she was aware that her husband and his superior, Superintendent Kevin Lennon, were involved in planting explosives purported to belong to subversive groups, with a view to then discovering them in an attempt to enhance their reputation and promotion prospects with their superiors.

On 26 April, 2000, a meeting was set up in Letterkenny General Hospital between Dr Barry, Professor Harbison and four senior officers attached to the Carty inquiry to discuss the exhumation. The post mortem report and available photographs were discussed at great length. Members of the Carty team asked the pathologists what could be gained, if anything, from exhuming the body. Dr Harbison felt that while an opportunity to examine the bones and skull may be of some help, it was unlikely that his findings would indicate the nature of how the injuries occurred. Dr Barry pointed out to the meeting that it would be less than proper to exhume a body, with the resulting trauma to family and friends, unless looking for something in particular that had not already been investigated. The conclusion was that exhumation was not warranted.

However, just over a year later, the Carty inquiry felt that in order to leave no stone unturned, it would again meet with Dr Harbison. This time he advised them that the only way to resolve the matters in relation to the death of Richie Barron was to examine the skull fractures. On 3 July, 2001, the Minister for Justice, John O'Donoghue, signed an order for the remains of Richie Barron to be exhumed.

On 6 July, 2001, Professor Harbison, the then State Pathologist, examined the remains, and noted that there were two groups of fractures to the skull, at the left skull base and the right frontal area, that is forehead to upper jaw.

'There can be no doubt that this left-side fragmentation was the result of very considerable force [which] would suggest that this was due to one massive impact, such as the left side of the back of the head striking the ground, though vehicular impact at this point cannot be totally excluded.'

Commenting on the fractures on the right side of the skull, Professor Harbison said, 'The most striking feature of this right-sided forehead fracture, and its difference from the fragmentation of the fracture on the left side, is the presence of some nine or ten gently curved scuff marks on the bone surface. These are 1¾ inches long and curve from below right upwards towards the left.' This indicates that Richie could have received a blow from a round instrument such as a bar or baton.

The current State Pathologist, Dr Marie Cassidy, also examined the partial remains of Richie Barron, and her findings are in accord with Dr Harbison. In her report she indicates there are two sides of impact to the head, and says that Richie Barron could have been hit a glancing blow or a side swipe by something projecting from a vehicle, causing the first injury, which then caused him to be propelled to the ground, causing the second, frontal injury.

***

When the Gardaí received the results of the initial post-mortem from Dr Barry, they decided to launch a full-scale murder investigation. An incident room was set up in Letterkenny Garda station. A conference was held on 15 October, 1996, which was chaired by Superintendent Fitzgerald, who had visited the scene earlier in the day. Those present were told to keep an open mind as they began the investigation.

Fitzgerald was still not satisfied that his earlier concerns regarding the behaviour of the four gardaí who attended the scene were properly noted. This prompted him to write an official report on the evening of 15 October, one day after Richie had been killed.

He again asked why it took Gardaí 35 minutes to respond to the call from Rita McBride reporting the incident, why the scene had not been preserved and why Garda Mulligan could not be contacted by radio.

On the evening before Richie Barron was killed, Garda Mulligan went on duty at 8 pm and was due to finish at 4 am the following morning. He was the only garda on duty in Raphoe that evening. According to Garda Boyce from the communications centre, he had been unable to contact Garda Mulligan on his radio at 1.05 am. Garda Mulligan claimed that he patrolled the village of Raphoe from 8 pm to 11.35 pm. He said he then returned to the station where he remained until Garda O'Dowd called to see him at 12.45 am. Then, according to his account, he went for a drive with Garda O'Dowd in O'Dowd's private car. At 1.15 am, Garda Mulligan saw two youths fighting outside McBrearty's nightclub, so he approached them and spoke with them. When he and O'Dowd returned to the centre of Raphoe, he spoke to local man, Stephen McCullagh, who informed him that Richie Barron had been knocked down.

At that stage, Mulligan and O'Dowd met with the two gardaí from Lifford, and accompanied them to the scene of the accident. O'Dowd confirmed Mulligan's account of that evening, and said that the reason he called to the station was to leave in some paperwork.

Garda Mulligan contacted Raphoe Station on 19 October, 1996, and said he was suffering from stress and was unfit for work. He stayed out sick for a period of 23 days.

Garda John O'Dowd is from Tubbercurry, Co. Sligo. He joined An Garda Síochána in October 1979. Six years later, at Buncranna District Court, he was convicted for having no car tax or insurance and was fined IR£120. In January 1996, he was posted to Raphoe on a temporary basis.

On the morning that Richie Barron was killed, Garda O'Dowd stopped a car which was being driven by Eamonn Strain, who had been at the cinema with his girlfriend, Anne Toye, earlier that evening. Eamonn Strain claims that he saw a car behind him flashing its lights and assumed it was a police car, however it was O'Dowd in his own car. When he pulled in, O'Dowd opened the passenger door, placed his knee on the passenger seat, identified himself and said, 'There was a poor ould c*** knocked down.' He also said it had been a hit-and-run accident. O'Dowd questioned Strain about his movements and asked him if he had been in Raphoe that night. He chatted to him for about five minutes and even told him not to be afraid.

What is significant about Eamonn Strain's account is that he claims that he was stopped at 12.45 am. When Garda O'Dowd was recalling this event, he wrongly claimed that Strains' girlfriend was in the car at the time. He would later admit that this may have been incorrect, yet he continues to maintain the time was 1.45 am, and not 12.45 am as stated by Eamonn Strain in his statement. Anne Toye's account is closer to her boyfriend's than that given by O'Dowd. She has no doubt that she was dropped off in time to be in her bed before 1 am. She was heading to Dublin with her mother the next day and was anxious to get home that evening. Garda O'Dowd claims that he stopped a number of vehicles in the Glenmaquinn area near the scene of death and that he went home at 4 am on the morning of 14 October, 1996. If the times given by Eamonn Strain and his girlfriend are correct, then O'Dowd discussed the death with Strain before the call notifying Gardaí of the accident had been made.

Neither Garda O'Dowd nor Garda Mulligan have ever accounted for their whereabouts at the time Richie Barron was killed, some time between 12.45 and 12.55 am on the morning of 14 October, 1996. The Carty report states: 'The question of the alleged Garda involvement in the death [of Richie Barron] is still under urgent investigation. The movements of Garda O'Dowd and Mulligan on the night of the death still have to be resolved.'

The two men have since changed information that they gave in their original statements.

On 16 September, 1999, Garda Mulligan gave a statement to the Carty inquiry. Although three years on, he said that his original statement about the time that Garda O'Dowd called to the station was wrong. He claimed that O'Dowd called at 11.45 pm on 13 October, 1996, and not 12.45 am on 14 October.

The Carty report states: 'In this further statement he still failed to address the issue of accounting for his whereabouts at the critical time.'

Investigating Gardaí from the Carty inquiry sought to interview Mulligan again on 26 October, 1999. On this occasion he was accompanied by a member of the Garda Representative Association (GRA). Mulligan was told that the Carty team wished to question him about his movements on the night of 13 October, 1996, and the early hours of the following morning. Garda Mulligan advised the investigators that he required time to consider their request. The following day he informed them that, having taken legal advice, he was refusing to answer any questions on this matter.

Carty's men were not giving up and wrote to Garda Mulligan again in November requesting that he give an account of his movements at the time Richie Barron was killed. Three months later, his solicitor replied saying that he advised his client not to answer any questions. They tried many more times to get Mulligan to give details of his movements, but to date he has refused.

Mulligan and O'Dowd were unaware at this stage that the investigators already knew they had been lying to them. Prior to their meeting with members of the Carty inquiry in May 2000, the investigators had already established that the two gardaí had been drinking in Daly's pub in Lifford between 11.30 pm and 12 am on

13 October, 1996. Another garda, Garda James Connolly, who recognised both men when he saw them in the pub, had passed this information to them.

On 8 May, 2000, officers called to Garda Mulligan at Letterkenny Garda station and had a meeting with him. They called again on 9 May, asked him to go to the place where Richie Barron had been killed and show them what he knew about the incident. Mulligan agreed, but stated that he wished to drive there alone. Three senior officers waited at the scene for him, and when he arrived, rather than being alone, he was with Garda O'Dowd. The officers expressed their surprise that O'Dowd was in attendance. It appeared to some of those involved that they were ensuring that they both gave the same account of what had happened at the scene that night.

While Mulligan and O'Dowd were at this meeting, they were informed that the investigators knew they had been lying about the night Richie Barron was killed, that there was a reliable witness who placed them both in Daly's pub in Lifford between 11.30 pm and 12 am. The two gardaí were asked to provide their cars for technical examination so that they could be ruled out of involvement in the death of Richie Barron. They were told that other issues needed clarification and a list of questions was prepared for both men to answer.

At the request of Garda Mulligan, his next meeting with members of the Carty team took place in a car park in Letterkenny, as he did not wish to meet with them at the police station. At this meeting, on Friday, 12 May, 2000, investigators provided Mulligan with a list of questions and told him they wanted a full statement by the following Tuesday.

One of the questions they asked concerned a call from Raphoe Garda station to the home of Garda John O'Dowd at 3.50 am on the morning Richie Barron was killed. This call had been made ten minutes before Garda Mulligan finished his shift. The Carty team were anxious to know what could have been so important to prompt a call at this hour of the morning.

However, statements were not forthcoming from Mulligan or O'Dowd. On 17 May, members of the inquiry team called and were informed that the two guards were working on their statements. They called again the following day, and noticed that Mulligan had the questions in front of him, so the officers were satisfied that he was finishing his statement. Later that evening, the Carty team received a call from Garda Martin Leonard of the GRA, who asked them to meet with him. At this meeting, Garda Leonard said that both Mulligan and O'Dowd would be handing their statements over later that evening, and would be accepting the witness account of the pub incident in full. He asked that they receive only a warning, rather than a more severe discipline. Garda Leonard advised the officers that the two gardaí were meeting their solicitor at 10 pm that night.

At 3.20 am the following morning, 19 May, 2000, Garda Mulligan reported sick and unfit for duty. At midday, a letter was faxed to Letterkenny Garda station from Mr P Dorrian, solicitor for both Mulligan and O'Dowd, stating that neither would be making any further statements and accusing the Carty investigation of intimidation.

The dealings that the Carty inquiry had with Garda O'Dowd practically mirror those they had with Mulligan, except that O'Dowd states that he has no recollection of receiving a phone call at his home at 3.50 am on the morning Richie Barron died. This call is recorded in the Telecom Eireann records.

The Carty inquiry noted:

> There is a serious conflict in accounts given by Eamonn Strain and Anne Toye on the one hand, and Garda O'Dowd on the other, and it is thought that John O'Dowd is not accurate in his account of events surrounding this incident.

Garda John O'Dowd reported unfit for duty on 24 April, 1999, and has not returned to work since.

Mulligan and O'Dowd submitted their cars for technical examination and no evidence was found to link either car to the crime scene. Because of their failure to co-operate with the inquiry, a notice of discipline was served on both men in July 2000. Their lack of co-operation left members of the Carty inquiry concerned that they had in fact something to hide, and bearing in mind the rumours at the time of Richie's death, they knew this would reflect badly on the force.

On 28 March, 2002, the Morris tribunal was set up by a resolution passed in the Dáil and by subsequent order of the Minister for Justice given on 24 April, 2002. The purpose of the tribunal is to have an independent inquiry into the allegations made concerning the behaviour of certain members of An Garda Síochána in the Donegal region. There are a number of serious issues being investigated and one of these is the circumstances surrounding the investigation into the death of Richie Barron. The Morris tribunal is expected to conclude its investigation into this matter in 2005.

***

Soon after the death of Richie Barron, Garda O'Dowd received information that led to Frank McBrearty Jr. and Mark McConnell becoming the prime suspects in the crime. It could be seen as significant that it was O'Dowd, who himself refuses to account for his movements at the crucial time, who turned the attention of the investigation onto two other men.

At 10 pm on the evening of 15 October, 1996, O'Dowd called Superintendent Denis Fitzpatrick, Divisional Director of the Donegal Division, at home. O'Dowd informed him he had obtained information that Mark McConnell and Frank McBrearty Jr., who were first cousins, had killed Richie Barron and that he had not died as a result of a hit-and-run accident. Chief Superintendent Fitzpatrick discussed the matter that night with Superintendent Fitzgerald, and the men agreed to meet at the scene the next morning.

Garda O'Dowd had received the information while interviewing Noel McBride about the theft in June 1996 of an aerial from the technical school in Raphoe. Noel McBride has a number of previous convictions and has served time in prison for larceny and criminal damage. He is well known to Gardaí in the region. Prior to interviewing McBride, Garda O'Dowd told members of the investigating team that he had information concerning the death of Richie Barron and that he wished to discuss this with Noel McBride. McBride told him that he saw Frank McBrearty Jr. and Mark McConnell coming up from rough ground at the back of Frankie's nightclub, which leads out to the place where Richie Barron was murdered.

For a number of weeks, senior Gardaí believed that the informer was a reliable person, who had given information to the Gardaí in the past, and were unaware that it was, in fact, Noel McBride.

It soon became known in Raphoe that Mark McConnell and Frank McBrearty Jr. were considered by the Gardaí to be suspects in what was now being treated as a murder case. On 27 October, 1996, just two weeks after the murder of Richie Barron, Frank McBrearty Sr. approached Garda O'Dowd and Garda Dan Curran and told them that people in Raphoe were calling him a murderer. The McBreartys were soon subjected to numerous abusive phone calls to their home and were the subject of much rumour in the town. Because of the bad blood that existed between the McBrearty and the Barron families, a lot of people believed these unfounded allegations.

The farcical situation that now existed is best described in the opening statement to the Morris tribunal, by senior counsel Peter

Charlton: 'Sir, we are now at a point which is one or two weeks after the death of Mr Barron. The Gardaí apparently have a murder investigation on their hands, but they do not have a report from a forensic pathologist [they did have the autopsy report from local pathologist Dr Barry within days of the death, but it would be a further four years before State Pathologist Dr Harbison submitted his first report on this matter, when asked for assistance by the Carty inquiry]. The Gardaí apparently believe that Mark McConnell and Frank McBrearty Jr. have murdered Richard Barron, but they do not have any evidence that Richard Barron was murdered ... Apparently they have a bald statement to that effect from Garda John O'Dowd ... It is nothing more than assertion because it contains absolutely no information as to how the crime was committed. Furthermore, it is completely lacking in any detail.'

Mr Charlton also points out that O'Dowd's statement should be totally dismissed because Noel McBride was not even in Raphoe on the night that Richie Barron was killed. He was attending a family function many miles away at the time in question. This is something that could have been easily clarified by the investigating team.

Superintendent Fitzgerald treated the McBride information with some caution. He claims that Chief Superintendent Fitzpatrick told him that Richie Barron had been murdered, and that Frank McBrearty Jr. and Mark McConnell did it. Fitzgerald, however, felt that they should investigate with an open mind. There were no questions asked in an attempt to ascertion where the information supplied by Noel McBride came from, but Superintendent Fitzgerald immediately assumed that it had come from Garda O'Dowd or Superintendent Lennon.

'I assumed that, because if it were anybody else I would have been told ... I did consider the information and decided not to mention it at the conference [held in Letterkenny station on 16 October, 1996, to discuss the case with the various officers involved], that it would be much better to allow the investigation to take its course, and I emphasised that people must approach that matter with an open mind. That information very soon spread and a Mr X was introduced by Garda O'Dowd as having been in the car park of Frankie's nightclub and putting Frankie Jr. and Mark McConnell there at the vital time. As time went on, I specifically requested at conference that a statement would have to be taken from this Mr X because I wanted corroboration of this information.'

***

During the following weeks and months, rumour spread about Raphoe and surrounding areas. There was a strong belief that because of the row on the night of 13 October between Mark McConnell and Richie Barron, Frank Jr. and Mark lay in wait for Richie and attacked him when he arrived at the fatal spot. The McBreartys started to receive abusive phone calls as did some of their relations. It would appear that calls attempting to extort money from the McBreartys' relations were made from the home of Garda O'Dowd. On 10 June, 1999, O'Dowd was arrested for his alleged involvement in these extortion calls and a file submitted to the DPP.

Michael and Charlotte Peoples are related to Mark McConnell. They received a number of calls to their home from the family home of a Garda informer and also from the home of Garda O'Dowd.

In a statement to police, Michael Peoples alleged the following, which has been established as correct in subsequent investigations: 'At approximately 8.05 pm on Saturday, 9 November, 1996, my wife Charlotte called me downstairs [saying] that I was wanted on the phone. I took the phone and a male voice asked me, "Are you

Michael Peoples? ... Remember the carry on that you were at on Saturday night?" I said, "What carry on?" He said, "You killed Richie Barron, I seen ya. I seen you and your wife outside the Parting Glass at twenty past one ... You drive a bread van and you're the only one in Raphoe who carries a baton in their van." I thought it was a wind-up. He said, "I seen ya, ya go running down the field, I seen ya hitting Richie Barron with the baton and running down the field ... You're going to Mountjoy, you'd better get your hole ready." He said, "I want money, I'm going to the Guards." I told him to fuck off and hung up the phone.

'At one stage during the conversation, Charlotte took the phone and asked the caller why he was doing this to us. About a half an hour later I answered the phone again. It was the same man on the phone. He asked me, "Are you going to take me serious?" I said, "Why don't you go to the Guards?" He said, "I was in a robbery that night and I left my fingerprints all over the place, that's why I can't go the Guards." We had a conversation for about three or four minutes and he demanded IR£2,000 ... I offered him IR£1,000. He said to meet him at the pub at the Whitecross with the money ... he would be wearing a black leather jacket, white Levis T-shirt and brown corduroys. I said I would meet him at 11 o'clock.

'At about 10.25 pm that same evening, the phone rang again. In the meantime I [had gotten] a small tape-recorder from a friend in Letterkenny. It was the same man again, I taped this conversation. He asked me, "Have you got the money?" I said, "I'll give you IR£500, I cannot raise more than that." He said, "I am not a hard man to bargain with you know." I said, "There'll be no trouble."

'This conversation lasted less than a minute. Just before 11 o'clock, myself and my father-in-law left the house in Charlotte's car and went to the Whitecross pub. I went into the pub and stayed a minute or so, but [didn't see anybody] fitting the description of the man. I went outside and waited a few minutes, three or four boys came out of the pub while I was there, but I didn't know any of them ... we came back home then.

'We had three calls in all that evening. My wife Charlotte answered the phone at 8.00 pm, but nobody answered when she lifted the phone. It was the same person on the phone the three times and he had a local accent.'

By this time, Noel McBride was telling more lies in an attempt to further implicate the McBreartys. He was alleging that Frank McBrearty Sr. was paying him to keep quiet. He claimed that he had received money from McBrearty Sr. and that McBrearty had bought a bike for his child. None of these allegations were true, but those who wanted to believe this did.

Senior officers involved in the inquiry formed the view in November 1996 that various people should be arrested concerning the death of Richie Barron. They formed this view on a number of grounds.

First, they took into account the information supplied by Garda O'Dowd that Frank McBrearty Jr. and his cousin Mark McConnell had been seen by Noel McBride in the car park of Frankie's nightclub about the time that Richie Barron died. Another Garda had received information from a local man that Frank McBrearty Jr. was seen in the company of two other men in the car park at the same time, and that the men seemed excited.

Senior Gardaí also took into account the lies told by Noel McBride, which they chose to believe at the time, that he had been induced by Frank McBrearty Sr. to withhold information from investigating Gardaí. There was also information that a call had been made by a relation of Mark McConnell to Letterkenny General Hospital enquiring as to the condition of Richie Barron. The investigating Gardaí were also aware of the verbal row between Mark McConnell and Richie Barron on the night Richie died.

Finally, Gardaí believed that a number of friends and relations of both Frank McBrearty Jr. and his cousin Mark McConnell were in possession of information that the two men were involved in the killing of Richie Barron. They formed this view because a number of friends of the suspects were in each other's company after the alleged assault was made against Richie Barron. Gardaí assumed that they were covering for McBrearty and McConnell.

A conference was held in Letterkenny Garda station on 3 December, 1996. The purpose of this conference was to discuss the arrests that were to be made the following day. It was attended by investigating Gardaí and also members of the Garda National Bureau of Criminal Investigation (GNBCI). The GNBCI were asked to assist because of the size of the proposed operation, and also because many of those who belong to this unit have experience in interviewing suspects involved in serious crime.

The meeting discussed the times that certain suspects would be arrested and made arrangements to have the children who may be with the suspects at the time of their arrest taken to family members. It was decided to arrest Frank McBrearty Jr. the next morning as he dropped his children to school. Why it was decided to arrest him on his way to the school, when his children were in the car, and not when he dropped them off, is only known to those who made the decision.

***

At 7.30 am on 4 December, 1996, a number of Gardaí went to Thorn Road in Letterkenny, where they set up a checkpoint with the purpose of arresting Frank McBrearty Jr. on route to the Raphoe National School. In all, seven Gardaí set out to the Thorn Road. A ban Garda, Tina Fowley, was there to look after the children after their father had been arrested.

At 9.20 am, Sergeant Joseph Hannigan arrested Frank McBrearty Jr. When he was stopped and told he was being arrested for the murder of Richie Barron, McBrearty became aggressive and annoyed. Gardaí say that his behaviour upset his children. McBrearty, however, claims that the Gardaí were the ones shouting, calling him names and upsetting his children. He was also concerned for his youngest child, who suffered from asthma, as he was worried that the boy would have an attack. Most of this confrontation and distress could have been avoided if the Gardaí had arrested McBrearty as he returned home, when his children were safely settled in school.

Peter Charlton SC in his opening statement to the Morris Tribunal claims that Frank McBrearty Jr. made the following allegations. McBrearty was placed in a patrol car and brought to Letterkenny Garda station. He claims that while in the back of the car he was assaulted, with Gardaí poking and punching him, while another Garda verbally abused him. Some Gardaí, however, complained about McBrearty's behaviour on the way to the station. Gardaí would have been aware that Frank McBrearty Jr. was a tough man. On 30 December, 1996, a man called Edward Moss complained to the Gardaí that he had been ejected from Frankie's niteclub. Moss claims that when he was removed from the club, he was beaten to the ground by three bouncers, and while he was on the ground, McBrearty continually beat his leg with a stick until his leg broke. Moss issued civil proceedings against McBrearty, but these charges were dropped when McBrearty paid him IR£15,000 in compensation.

When they arrived at Letterkenny Garda station, Sergeant Hannigan advised the member in charge why McBrearty had been arrested. McBrearty was then advised of his rights and he signed the custody record. At this stage McBrearty was in handcuffs and complaining that they were too tight. He claims that Sergeant Hannigan wanted to remove the handcuffs, but two detectives said, 'Leave the handcuffs on the murdering bastard.'

McBrearty was then brought to an interview room and claims that on the way there he was constantly punched in the back by

Detective Garda Keating, who was told to stop hitting him by Inspector McGinley. Keating and McGinley then handed him over to four detectives from the GNBCI. The four who had the task of interviewing Frank McBrearty Jr. were detectives John Melody, John Fitzpatrick, Gerard McGrath and Eamonn O'Grady.

Detectives O'Grady and McGrath carried out the first interview. It would appear from all the notes taken during his detention that McBrearty stuck with his original story, that he'd had nothing to do with the death of Richie Barron and had not been in the vicinity of the crime scene all night. The only time that this version of events changed was in a confession that he denies ever making and claims was forged.

The following is an extract of text from a memo of that first interview, as noted by Gardaí:

Detective: [Informs McBrearty of his rights and asks him was he aware of the reason why he was arrested.]

McBrearty: Yes. This is a load of shite lads. I am an innocent man.

Detective: We are investigating the murder of Richie Barron at Townparks, Raphoe, Co. Donegal, on the morning of 14 October, 1996. We believe you were involved in this crime.

McBrearty: I don't know anything about it. It's shite lads. I had nothing to do with it. I should not be here. I am going to sue you all. It's all lies.

Detective: Information in our possession suggests that you and Mark McConnell carried out this murder.

McBrearty: That's not true. I never hit any man in my life and Mark is a very civil man who would do no harm to any man.

Detective: Were you in the car park of Frankie's at any time during that night?

McBrearty: No. I was not near the car park. I'm innocent.

Detective: Are you sure about this?

McBrearty: I am telling you the truth. I was not there.

Detective: We have a witness who states that he saw you up in Frankie's car park on the morning of 14 October at approximately 1 am.

McBrearty: That's lies, you don't believe the gobshites of Raphoe, they're all against us.

Detective: Were you accompanied by Mark McConnell at this time you were first seen by this witness at the rusty barrels of Frankie's car park?

McBrearty: That's all lies. I wasn't with Mark McConnell or nobody else. I am telling you now, you can't believe anyone from Raphoe. It's a wicked community out there, and you would want to come out and live out there. Everybody is at each other's throat.

Detective: So this witness is lying?

McBrearty: Yes, he is fucking lying. I'm an innocent man. They're all jealous of us.

Detective: Were you at the scene where Richard Barron's body was found on the morning of 14 October?

McBrearty: No. I was not. I did not leave Frankie's that night. I was working there from 8 pm to 3.30 am in the morning.

Detective: Could you have been seen up there [where Richie Barron was found]?

McBrearty: I was not there. Nobody saw me.

Detective: Are you sure about this?

McBrearty: I know I wasn't seen there.

Detective: Why? Did you check to see whether there was anyone else around when this murder was carried out?

McBrearty: I'm not saying any more. You're trying to put words in my mouth.

At this stage it was now 10.20 am. Frank's solicitor arrived at the station and requested to see his client and the interview was adjourned for 30 minutes. The questioning resumed when the two detectives returned at 10.50 am and advised Frank Jr. that he was still under caution.

Detective: Did you carry out this murder?

McBrearty: [Aren't] I telling you lads, I had nothing to do with it.

Detective: We have evidence that you were involved in this murder.

McBrearty: Well show me then, where is the proof? [You] have nothing lads and I know it. Them rhinestone cowboys out there have made a shite of it.

Detective: There were over 500 statements taken in this investigation and no stone was left unturned.

McBrearty: It's all shite, I am telling [you], they're all liars.

Detective: What is your relationship with your father?

McBrearty: I love my daddy, I would have nothing without him.

Detective: Is that why he interfered with witnesses who made statements to the Gardaí about the events of 14 October?

McBrearty: That's all wrong. He was asking what the guards were saying that's all. He is that kind of man, he gets involved, he is paranoid.

Detective: Did he not want the Gardaí to investigate this crime?

McBrearty: I am sick with him. He was told to leave the guards alone.

Detective: Did he tell you about this?

McBrearty: My father tells me nothing, he doesn't even tell me how much money he has in the bank.

Detective: This intimidation started on the night of 14 October when your father pulled his car in behind one of the witnesses in Raphoe that night and put his full headlights on the witness's vehicle.

McBrearty: That's lies. I'm telling you, you don't believe the people from Raphoe. They're liars.

Detective: Why would your father do that?

McBrearty: I'm not answering any more questions about my daddy, it's got nothing to do with him.

Detective: Did you and Mark McConnell murder Richie Barron?

McBrearty: That's shite. I'm an innocent man.

Detective: How did you get on with Richard Barron?

McBrearty: I know him. I don't like the man, there's no point in saying that. My father talks to him.

Detective: You were upset when Richie told Mark McConnell in Quinn's (Town and Country) that he was some excuse for a McBrearty.

McBrearty: That's shite, I didn't hear about the row for three days afterwards. I didn't see Richie Barron that night.

Detective: Did you murder Richie Barron?

McBrearty: I'm an innocent man, the whole thing is shite. I'm innocent, no matter what you say.

Detective: Did a witness not see you in the car park of Frankie's at 1 am on the night of 14 October?

McBrearty: Say whatever you like, look up the evidence. I wasn't seen there. I told you that.

Detective: When did you first hear about Richie Barron being killed?

McBrearty: Michelle Scott told me that Richie was after being hit, she said he was after being knocked down.

Detective: Did you do that hitting?

McBrearty: I'm an innocent man.

McBrearty agreed to have his prints taken, and gave hair and blood samples. However, when the notes of this interview were read over to him, he refused to sign them as his solicitor had told him not to sign anything. The interview concluded when the member in charge entered the room and told the interviewers that the prisoner should be allowed a period of rest.

Very serious allegations are made against the officers who carried out the interviews with McBrearty. He alleges that the officers accused him of not caring for his wife or children, and said that he was brain damaged as a result of beatings his father gave him when he was growing up. He claims that Sergeant Melody continually poked him and that Fitzpatrick pulled his hair and ear. Both are alleged to have said to him, 'Come on admit you're a murderer, you're a murderer, you're a murderer.'

At one stage a scuffle broke out when Detective Garda Fitzpatrick grabbed McBrearty, but then, according to McBrearty, he put Fitzpatrick over the table telling him not to try his strength against his.

In one of the afternoon interviews, McBrearty claims that he was shown a statement which he was told had been made by Mark McConnell admitting to their involvement in the murder of Richie Barron. McBrearty claims he knew this was a lie because the name McConnell was spelt incorrectly. Many allegations were made against McBrearty and he continued to protest his innocence. At the conclusion of the third interview, Melody and Fitzpatrick noted the following:

Detective: You should consider telling us the truth and make a written statement about what happened that night. Do you understand?

McBrearty: I'll think about it.

This interview concluded at 6.15 pm and again McBrearty refused to sign the notes. He complains that he was then assaulted a second time.

At 7 pm, Detectives Melody and Fitzgerald returned to interview McBrearty again, but what would normally be regarded as a major breakthrough ended up being a major embarrassment to the Gardaí. The two gardaí claim that McBrearty confessed to killing Richie Barron that night. The following is a text of that confession:

'Listen, I'll tell you what happened on the 14th of October, 1996. I heard that Richard Barron was up to his old tricks again, mouthing about the McBreartys, Mark McConnell, he's my first cousin, told me this. He had a row with him in Quinn's (Town and Country) pub that evening. His wife Róisín was also there. Mark was very annoyed over the row and what Richard Barron said to him.

'When he came over to the club, that is Mark McConnell, he told me that he had seen Richie off at the top of the road. We went up the back way across the car park and got on to the main road. We waited for Richie Barron there. We intended having a word with him. We saw Richie coming, he was on his own. I picked up a bit of timber.

'When we stopped him, he lashed out at us, but he missed. I hit him a slap on the head, and he fell back. We then ran. I dropped the timber I had on the way back. We got into the club, and it was not until later that I heard that Richie had been knocked down by a hit-and-run. Michelle Scott told me. My father found out about what happened and he said he would look after it for us. *My father never intimidated anyone. He never offered, to my knowledge, money to anyone to not give evidence against me. This statement has been read over to me and is correct.'*

This is a very significant document. It was a major breakthrough in the case, yet it was not reported to the DPP. McBrearty denies that he made this statement and claims that he only made the comments at the end that are in italics. It transpires that the part of the statement in italics is on the second side of a two-page statement, and all of the incriminating comments are detailed on the first side of the page, which is not initialled or signed by Frank McBrearty.

There are also other points that should be noted. The Gardaí already had statements that showed that Michelle Scott did not tell McBrearty that Richie Barron had been knocked down. The suggestion that she did is an error, and was one made in an earlier statement by McBrearty. There were many accounts of Richie Barron that night and all of these would suggest that he would have been too intoxicated to lash out at his attackers. Had he tried to hit them, he would have fallen to the road. Furthermore, the evidence of the pathologist does not tie in with Richie being hit on the head with an instrument such as a piece of timber. Also, no piece of timber was ever found at the scene.

There are other issues that call into question the credibility of the alleged confession. It was not consistent with McBrearty's behaviour. He had been denying his involvement all along and had refused to sign most records of meetings put before him. Also, other officers involved in the investigation were not even informed of this huge development.

More importantly, Garda Martina Fowley, who was involved in the incident room, claims that officers from GNBCI had practised McBrearty's signature and even asked her if it was a good copy.

In a statement she made to her superiors on 13 October, 1999, Garda Fowley said: 'On 4 December, 1996, I was on duty at Letterkenny Garda station. I was detailed for duty in the incident room. There were a number of persons in custody in connection with the murder of Richard Barron, including two of the main suspects at the time, namely Mark McConnell and Frank McBrearty Jr. During the course of the afternoon I was present in the conference room with Sergeant Roache and Inspector John McGinley.

'Inspector John McGinley was sitting at the conference table facing toward the door ... He was writing on an official half sheet. I had cause to retrieve some papers from this table. In doing so I passed behind. He turned to me and showed me the half sheet of paper he had been writing on ... There was writing on this sheet of paper covering approximately a third of the page. There was also the name of Frank McBrearty written in longhand at the end of this writing. Also on the table in front of Inspector McGinley was a black and white photocopy of a manuscript signature of the name Frank McBrearty. From my recollection this signature was on a photocopy of a C84 form [a form a prisoner signs to acknowledge that he has been advised of his rights].

'Inspector McGinley showed me the half sheet and asked me was "that a good likeness?" I took this to mean were both signatures alike. I thought this was a practical joke, I started laughing and so did he. I returned to my seat and Inspector McGinley left the room with the papers he had been working on shortly after.

'Sergeant Roache asked me what was all that about. I told him [Inspector McGinley] wanted to know if what he had written was a good copy of Frank McBrearty's signature. Sergeant Roache dismissed it as a joke and commented that it was another one of his pranks. I took it to be a ruse and thought no more about it until recently when concerns about the veracity of the statement of admission obtained had been expressed in the public media.'

Garda Fowley concluded her statement saying, 'This report is submitted to ease my conscience and uphold the integrity of our force. It is made without malice towards any individual personalities. While feeling duty compelled to report my concerns on these matters, I sincerely hope that the fears I have expressed are found to be groundless.'

This most serious allegation by Garda Fowley was subsequently investigated by the Carty inquiry. It was taken seriously enough that the statement was sent overseas for independent expert analysis. The report prepared by forensic expert Dr Kim Harry Hughes suggested that the signature and three lines on the second page were written on an uneven surface. There was no evidence of this being the case on the other side, which contained the incriminating confession.

At a meeting held with two officers, Inspector Hugh Coll and Detective Sergeant Jim Fox, on 13 October 1999, Frank McBrearty Jr. summed up his main complaints against the Gardaí. McBrearty's biggest complaint was the manner of his arrest – in front of his children while he brought them to school. He also complained that he had been physically assaulted and said that one detective had beaten him and burned him with cigarettes. He was adamant that he had made no confession, and said that he hoped the body of Richie Barron would be exhumed as he felt that this would prove his innocence.

McBrearty claims that there were a lot of Gardaí in Raphoe that night and that one of them hit Richie Barron with his car at the cinema and then moved his body to where it had been discovered. This was one of the rumours that was circulating about Raphoe in the days following Richie's death.

***

On the same morning that Frank McBrearty Jr. was arrested, so too was Mark McConnell and his wife Róisín. When the Gardaí called to arrest McConnell at his home at 9.15 am, he was looking after his eighteen-month-old son, Dean. According to McConnell, the gardaí tried to take his child from him, but he resisted, and after some argument they allowed him to drive to his mother's so she could mind Dean while he was detained. Before he left his mother's house, he asked her to contact his solicitor and advise him about what was happening. The garda charged with the task of arresting McConnell was John O'Dowd.

There were a number of reasons why Gardaí claim it was appropriate to arrest McConnell. First, there was the argument with Richie Barron in the Town and Country public house. The Gardaí claimed that this created a motive for McConnell to kill Richie Barron. Second, there was the flawed information, which had been supplied to Garda John O'Dowd, that McConnell was observed at the car park in Frankie's nightclub close to where the body of Richie Barron had been found. Finally, there were alleged discrepancies in the statements given earlier by McConnell and his wife Róisín about phone calls on the night Richie Barron was killed.

Mark McConnell claims that he was assaulted and terrorised while in Garda custody. Detective Sergeant James Leahy and Garda Michael O'Malley conducted the first interview at 9.20 am. McConnell claims that during this interview, O'Malley was very aggressive, roaring and shouting at him and calling him a 'murdering bastard'. O'Malley told him that would never see his wife again.

At a later interview by other detectives, McConnell recalls: 'Detective Tague was the first guard to produce post-mortem photographs of Richie Barron. I refused to look at them ... He bent my ear to force me to look at them ... Another time he pulled my hair to make me look at them ... One time he came close up to my face and called me a murdering bastard. He spat in my face. Detective Tague punched me in the side with his fist. He kept poking me in the eye.'

As the period of detention came to an end, McConnell claims that four detectives came into the room. He maintains that they produced a statement that they said was a confession by Frank McBrearty Jr., which was then read over to him.

According to McConnell, the statement began with the words: 'I, Frank McBrearty Jr., am showing remorse for what I have done.'

The statement continued that he and McConnell had gone up the road to where Richie Barron was and had killed him. McConnell asked if he could look at the statement and when he saw it he knew straight away it had been forged because he was familiar with McBrearty's signature and knew that the one he was looking at was false. At this stage he realised that the detectives were lying to him.

McConnell had met with his solicitor for forty minutes that morning and, therefore, took the advice he had been given not to make a statement while in custody.

That same morning Róisín McConnell set out to the Fruit of The Loom factory in Raphoe, where she was employed as a machinist, with her colleagues. As she was travelling to work in a friend's car, she was stopped at a checkpoint and then was brought to Letterkenny Garda station.

It appears that the arrest of Róisín McConnell should never have occurred, as she herself was not suspected of the murder of Richie Barron. She was suspected of being an accessory to the murder, having knowledge of her husband's involvement and protecting him so that he could evade justice. However, the rule of common law is that a married woman does not become an accessory after the fact to a felony committed by her husband by receiving him, that is, giving him protection knowing he has committed a crime. This being the case, it is difficult to see how the arrest of Róisín McConnell could have been lawful.

When Róisín was brought to Letterkenny Garda station she was denied permission to make a telephone call, even though she was entitled to do so, and had been assured on the journey to the station that she would be allowed.

On 5 November, 2004, the state settled a legal action taken by Róisín Mc Connell as a result of her detention by officers investigating the death of Richie Barron. Róisín received settlement of €260,000 and her legal costs will also be paid. These are believed to be in excess of €500,000. In her statement of claim, she says that the manner of her detention and the intimidation, terrorising tactics and methods of interrogation used by the Gardaí have caused her immense damage. She claims that while in custody she was forced to pray to her late father asking him for forgiveness for the killing of Richie Barron. She states that she was pushed about, was constantly screamed at and was accused of being a member of the IRA. During one interview, the post-mortem photographs of Richie Barron were pushed into her face and she was forced to look at them. As this was happening, the lights were being turned on and off.

Róisín claims that detectives then told her that she would never see her young son again. She was told that her husband was unfaithful and was involved with other women. She was also told that her husband was responsible for the killing of Richie Barron. Róisín claims that Sergeant John White placed his backside close to her and broke wind in her face in an effort to humiliate and degrade her.

Róisín McConnell has suffered more than most because of the action of the Gardaí. Within two weeks of her arrest, she was admitted to Letterkenny Psychiatric Hospital where she complained of feeling extremely anxious. She believed that Satan had taken over her mind and was controlling her. She was extremely depressed and even considered suicide. When Róisín was first admitted to hospital she did so of her own free will, but her condition continually deteriorated and soon she refused to accept the help she needed. Her status changed from a voluntary patient to an involuntary patient under the Mental Treatment Act. She was detained in hospital as she was considered a risk to herself, and remained there for four weeks.

On her release, Róisín was placed on strong medication and has since developed acute paranoid psychosis. She cannot have a normal relationship with her young son, who she finds it difficult to cope with. Róisín has been advised that because of her medication, she will not be able to have any more children. Prior to her arrest on 4 December, 1996, Róisín had no previous history of psychiatric illness. She was employed, enjoyed a happy relationship with her husband and looked forward to rearing her family.

***

A number of other people were also arrested around the same time in connection with the case. These included Frank McBrearty Sr., who was accused of attempting to pervert the course of justice. Tensions in the town were running high as opinion was split in two – those who supported the McBreartys, and those who felt that they were guilty of the murder of Richie Barron.

Gardaí, who in the course of six months after the murder had served in excess of 150 summonses on the McBrearty's licensed premises over licensing laws, were also targeting the McBreartys. These summonses were subsequently dismissed and withdrawn by the Gardaí. Frank McBrearty Sr. feared for his family and was convinced that the Gardaí were unfairly intimidating them. He believed that his son was being accused of a murder that he did not commit, and that others were being targeted because they were related to the McBrearty family.

Frank McBrearty Sr. felt that the Gardaí investigation was not going to discover what really happened to Richie Barron on the night he died, because they had already made up their minds that his son and nephew were guilty. He decided that the only way to put an end to this situation, which was destroying their lives, was to call in his own investigators and solve this mystery himself. This course of action would cost tens of thousands of pounds, but to Frank Sr. the money was not an issue, protecting his family was his main concern. This was not the first time Frank Sr. had faced problems of this nature. While living in Scotland, he had been involved in an accident that resulted in his being charged with culpable homicide. He was not convicted of the charge and, soon after, returned to Ireland. It was because of this incident that people spoke about Frank Sr. getting off on murder charges in Scotland.

On 5 February, 1997, Frank McBrearty Sr. contacted a firm of private detectives. McBrearty told the firm that Gardaí were accusing his son Frank Jr. and his nephew Mark McConnell of murdering Richie Barron on the morning of 14 October, 1996. He also advised the detectives that he (Frank Sr.) was being accused of perverting the course of justice. Frank Sr. asked them to carry out an investigation into what happened that night as he felt it was now the only way he would prove his son's innocence. He assured the private detectives that he and his family were innocent of all allegations being made against them.

The arrival of private investigators on the scene did nothing to help the atmosphere in the deeply divided town of Raphoe. The new McBrearty funded investigation soon ran into difficulty as it was not receiving co-operation from the Barron family or their relations. This is not surprising as one would not expect them to co-operate with a firm working for those who they believed murdered their loved one.

In a detailed statement to the Garda Commissioner dated 18 June, 1997, one of the investigators said, 'I instructed one of my staff to approach the local parish priest Father McGettigan to advise the Barron family that I was happy with my investigation and that neither Mark McConnell nor Frank McBrearty Jr. had anything to do with the death of Richard Barron.'

The private investigators also requested that Father McGettigan ask the family of Richie Barron for their co-operation. They were most surprised to hear from the parish priest that the Barrons had been advised by the Gardaí that the case was over as they had detected the men responsible for Richie's murder.

The Barron family were told that the Gardaí had a confession from Frank McBrearty Jr. A number of other families who were approached by private investigators also refused to co-operate with their investigation.

In a statement, which was also forwarded to the Minister for Justice amongst others, one of the investigators talks about a close friend who is a serving member of the Gardaí. This friend told him that secret meetings were held in Northern Ireland during which serving members of the force complained about the Garda investigation and the manner in which people arrested during the Barron investigation were treated. The private detective claimed that when he met this friend on two separate occasions, he showed serious reservations about how this investigation would reflect on the force.

The private investigator maintained that there was a conspiracy to frame the McBreartys for the murder of Richie Barron and that, according to his unnamed acting Garda source, 'Senior members of the Gardaí responsible for the investigation into the death of Richard Barron absolutely hate Frank McBrearty Sr. because he was responsible for the dismissal from the force of a previous acting garda sergeant who attempted to extort money from Frank McBrearty.'

However, the Gardaí had formed their own view about the private investigation which was being funded by the McBreatry family. They were aware that over 150 statements had been gathered by this investigation in the Raphoe area. The Gardaí believed that this investigation was not acting to find the killers or establish what had happened, but was working to hinder the Gardaí as they went about their work.

The Carty inquiry, which had some of the most respected investigators in the state working for it, also made a number of observations concerning the McBrearty funded investigation. It said that a large number of the statements taken by this investigation lacked detail, were poorly taken, badly phrased and fell far short of the type of clarity required to verify the information supplied. The Carty inquiry found that it was evident from the behaviour of the private investigation that it was endeavouring to manipulate the Garda investigation to suit the purpose of its employer.

Furthermore, there were serious allegations being made against one of the private investigators who was employed by the McBreartys. A local man, Eugene Gamble, had made a statement to the Gardaí concerning people he had seen on the night Richie Barron died. One of these was Mark McConnell. Gamble alleges that one of the investigators made a number of calls to his house, and told him he was wrong about the time he claimed to have seen the people in Raphoe. Gamble insisted that he was correct. He claims that the investigator told him that he would make it worth his while if he changed his statement. Gamble asked the man who he was working for and was told that it was a private investigation being carried out on behalf of the McBreartys. According to various relatives of Gamble, this investigator also asked them what it would take to get Gamble to change his statement, and they understood that he was offering money.

Gardaí saw fit to interview this investigator concerning these serious allegations. Gardaí met him at his office where he was cautioned. When the Gardaí expressed their concerns and made him aware of the allegations, he declined to make any response. He informed the investigating gardaí that he would consider the allegations and reply at a later date. Following consultations with his solicitor he has declined to address any of the issues raised.

The Gardaí do not like private detectives working alongside them on investigations, and felt on a number of occasions that this privately funded investigation was going too far. However, they recognise it as a person's right to hire private investigators if they so wish. Not wanting to be seen as impinging further on the rights of the McBreartys, the Gardaí often turned a blind eye to this investgation's methods.

***

So what should have been a straightforward inquiry into how Richie Barron died in the early hours of 14 October, 1996, has now turned into one of the most expensive investigations in the history of the state. The Morris tribunal is investigating the death of Richie Barron and the Garda investigation of it, both of which were also thoroughly investigated by the Carty inquiry, yet the cause of Richie Barron's death is still unknown.

The Carty inquiry stated in its conclusions:

> It is of concern that it has not been possible to definitely establish how Richard Barron met his death. The investigation team have a great sympathy for the Barron family and respect the dignified manner in which they have responded to the intense media in the case. The allegations surrounding the arrest of suspects and the subsequent developments have been distressing for the family.
>
> There are many unanswered questions which must be resolved. The question of the alleged Garda involvement in the death is still under urgent investigation. The movements of Gardaí O'Dowd and Mulligan on the night of the death still have to be resolved.

There is no doubt that the reputation of the Gardaí has suffered due to what has been learned about certain activities in the Donegal region. It must not be forgotten, though, that it was the Gardaí and no one else who investigated and exposed the alleged corruption, and for that they must be admired. It shows that the vast majority of members of An Garda Síochána are honest and determined to stamp out crime and corruption, regardless of who is guilty. If in the interests of justice they have to expose colleagues who have broken the law or who have acted in an unprofessional way, then at least we can be confident that, regardless of the backlash to the force, there will be no cover ups.

On 31 July, 2000, Assistant Commissioner Kevin Carty said the following when presenting the findings of his investigation:

> This investigation has disclosed that a small number of Gardaí acted in an unethical and some cases a criminal manner; this is obviously a very serious matter, which needs to be addressed swiftly and decisively. The type of behaviour detailed in this report is not indicative of the Garda force in the Donegal Division. Over the past number of months there has been considerable pressure on the Divisional Force due to the media and political interest in this investigation. The members have responded to the challenge and continued to discharge their duties in a professional manner. The vast majority of the members are appalled at the allegations and have assisted in every way possible with this investigation.

Richie Barron's family had to endure further suffering when his body was exhumed in the hope much-wanted answers would be found. The McBreartys have also suffered, accused as they were for a death that we still do not know was murder. One young woman has seen her life destroyed and can no longer enjoy a normal relationship with her husband and child. All of this may have been avoided had the four gardaí who first arrived at the scene taken the proper steps. If they had done so, a lot of people could have been saved unnecessary pain and suffering. Most importantly, the family of Richie Barron has been denied closure, the death of Richie is constantly before them, as allegations and counter-allegations are made. They have not been afforded what is their right – an opportunity to let Richie rest in peace.

5

Veronica Guerin

A ruthless, well-organised criminal gang of drug lords, who believed they were untouchable, murdered journalist Veronica Guerin, a young mother, on 26 June, 1996. There has never been a murder in Ireland that created such a reaction and caused such outcry. The investigation into her death was the largest murder inquiry ever held in Ireland. Books have been published, TV programmes made, a film produced and many square miles of newsprint articles printed about Veronica, her life and her death. I have watched and observed, spoken out when necessary and tried at all times to co-operate with all of the above media, in an effort to have an accurate picture of Veronica painted and her story told correctly. Sometimes I have failed, but more often I have succeeded.

Veronica Guerin was my sister and this is my story.

I will show Veronica as she was, because I am proud of who she was. There will be no need to protect her, because she had nothing to hide. I am not a jealous colleague who feels that she had no right to be working in journalism. I have no axe to grind, no desire to destroy her character, and no necessity to please an editor or political handler who wants to besmirch Veronica's memory.

If when writing about events that followed Veronica's death I come across as bitter, it is because I am. If when writing about her former colleagues I come across as saddened, it is because I am. Some of these colleagues assassinated her character with the only apparent reason being that she eclipsed them in their chosen profession. If when talking about those who murdered her you cannot sense forgiveness on my part, it is because there is none. It may seem that I am availing of this opportunity to settle some old scores, this is true, but not my scores, only scores that I feel should be settled for Veronica.

If any person I believe to have been unkind to Veronica in the aftermath of her death is offended by my setting the record straight, I know that they have the opportunity to defend themselves should they feel they need. This opportunity was never afforded to Veronica, but unlike the lies told about her in death, I will only deal with the truth.

***

Veronica's murder is a direct attack on democracy in Ireland: a free press is essential to a free society, and the people who assassinated Veronica are trying to murder the freedom to investigate and report the truth about our society.

Sir Antony O Reilly, Independent Newspapers, 26 June, 1996

Veronica entered journalism late in life after trying out a number of careers, including one in The Credit Union. She also spent years working in our father's accountancy practice, where she remained until his unexpected death in 1981. From here she went to work at the New Ireland forum as an assistant to Charles J Haughey, one of Ireland's most controversial politicians who had been Taoiseach, but was then leader of the opposition.

Haughey appointed Veronica to this job, not just because he liked her, but because he knew Veronica was a woman of many talents and great ability. She also possessed the one quality that he admired most – loyalty.

Ours was a Fianna Fáil household and our father had been a lifelong supporter of Charles J Haughey. He believed that

Haughey was an exceptional politician who cared about people and who had the talent to make the difference. Our mother did not share this passion and admiration for him though. However, like most families at that time, we took the lead from our parents so we also supported Fianna Fáil.

I joined Fianna Fáil in 1977 and soon after I also joined Ógra Fianna Fáil. The following year, Veronica also joined Ógra and became very active in the Party. She had great admiration for Haughey. Veronica had strong views on the National Question and felt that Haughey was strong on this issue. She believed he provided a real chance of bringing about a situation that would result in a united Ireland. ·

As a member of the Party, Veronica worked tirelessly on Haughey's behalf in the many elections that were held throughout this period. Because of her bubbly personality and her ability to get along with people, she soon became recognised as one of the best canvassers in the Party. She seemed to have the ability to win over the undecided, and indeed talked many of them into helping the Party at election time. It was during an election that she met her husband, Graham Turley, and also became friendly with the Haughey children.

Veronica's dedication soon came to the attention of Haughey. The Fianna Fáil Party Leader enjoyed the stories that were relayed to him about Veronica's significant contribution during the various elections that were held during the late 1970s and early 1980s. It was at this time that Veronica acquired her first taste for writing. When the election newsletters were being produced, Veronica would write articles late into the evening, checking the content with election staff. While the rest of us would head for the pub following an evening's canvas, she would be making sure that matters that were coming up on the doorsteps were included in election material.

In May 1998, *Magill* magazine suggested in an article that Veronica voted on 27 occasions during the 1982 general election.

This is totally untrue. Like everyone else, Veronica had only one vote, but had she been inclined to participate in impersonating, it is more likely that the number of votes cast would have exceeded 100. I do know that one person cast 114 votes that day, and this person now holds the record for casting the most votes in a twelve-hour period in Dublin North Central.

During this period, impersonation played a big part in elections, particularly in Dublin North Central. A system had developed over the years that if a member of the Party was unable to cast their vote at election time, then his or her voting card would be handed in to Noel Dore, who was responsible for running the tally for Fianna Fáil at the election count. Noel, who died in 2004, was married to Haughey's sister, Bridie, who was secretary of the Fianna Fáil Dublin North Central Organisation for over 20 years.

Noel Dore was delighted with Veronica's overall performance during the 1982 election. He had no voting cards left when the polls closed. This was a major success and the fact that so many 'number ones' had been cast in the name of Charles J Haughey was a contributory factor in him increasing his number one vote in that election. One person had achieved the record that day, but not without many close encounters.

This impersonation machine stopped when Haughey's election agent and close friend, solicitor Pat O'Connor, and his daughter Niamh, who worked in the Fianna Fáil press office, were accused of voting twice. When people saw the trouble Pat O'Connor went to in order to avoid conviction, they decided that the risk of impersonating voters was too great, even for Haughey.

After the 1982 election, Haughey appointed Veronica to the Board of NIHE, which is now Dublin City University. She was a very proud and active member of the first board of this wonderful university. In 1984, when the New Ireland Forum was being created and Haughey was leader of the opposition, he appointed Veronica secretary to the Fianna Fáil group at the Forum. This was

Veronica's first serious appointment by Haughey, an appointment that was deeply resented by a number of people who were already working in the Party and had hoped to secure this important role.

Haughey knew that Veronica would be committed and give the hours and dedication that a job at the New Ireland Forum required. He was very aware that Veronica had good contacts in the media, and on occasions used her to leak information to journalists. While Haughey would publicly claim to be annoyed that certain details of discussions concerning the New Ireland Forum were being leaked to the media, it suited his agenda. Many years later, when discussing Haughey and the media, Veronica told me that it was he who had instigated the leaks. She did not mind being used, seeing this as part of her job. Haughey wanted something done and Veronica was keen to deliver.

People always unfairly suspected that Veronica was solely responsible for these leaks. Because of this, the question would be raised as to where she got the information. She knew the truth, as did Haughey, the Party Leader. However, stories soon spread about her being caught going through Haughey's personal papers, which some journalists suggested contributed to a cooling off between Veronica and Haughey, but this is totally untrue. First, if any person who knows anything about Haughey thinks that he would have tolerated such behaviour and allowed Veronica to remain in her position, they are not only being naïve, but also dishonest. Second, had this been the case, there were enough people who resented the close relationship that Veronica enjoyed with Haughey who would have welcomed the chance to damage it, along with Veronica's reputation, by leaking the information to the media.

What people fail to realise is that with Veronica, loyalty was absolute, anything less was not good enough. The commitment she showed to Haughey was the way she always acted, and she approached every job in the same way, always remaining loyal to her employer.

Less than a year after Veronica's death, Emily O'Reilly, who was then a journalist with *The Sunday Business Post*, began to write a book about Veronica which was to contain a lot of inaccurate and untrue stories that she had been told. I spent a lot of time convincing her that stories she intended to include were incorrect. If I persuaded her that something would be proven wrong or discredited then it wasn't incorporated into this character assassination of Veronica.

I became aware that one of Emily's main sources for the book was a former employee in Fianna Fáil. This person had relayed to Emily the untrue story of Veronica going through Haughey's personal papers and leaking information to the media while working on the New Ireland Forum, and this account was to be included in the book.

This former employee also fed Emily a story that concerned Veronica seeking help for her son Cathal, who was named after Charles Haughey, when in fact none was sought. The lie goes that Veronica told Haughey that Cathal was unwell and needed treatment overseas. It was obvious to all that Cathal was a well child and if Veronica had needed help, her family would have been her first port of call.

I knew that these lies would be damaging to Veronica's memory and I felt I had to act. In my view there was only one person who could rubbish this damaging allegation and prevent it from being included in Emily's book. That person was Haughey.

I contacted Haughey and arranged to meet him at his home. I expressed my concerns about the information that I knew was about to be published in Emily's book, and explained to him that he was the one person who could refute these claims. We discussed these issues at great length and he told me that, in his view, they would be best dealt with when the book came out. We discussed the fact that other allegations were being made in the book, which, although untrue, would not be as easy to disprove. It was agreed that when the book was published, Haughey would then speak out, and with the most serious allegations disproved, the rest of the book would be discredited. Haughey assured me that this would be done. I came away from that meeting delighted with his decision, but I was soon to learn that because of all the controversy surrounding Haughey at the time of the various tribunals, he took the decision that it would be unwise for him to involve himself in this debate.

When Emily's book was published amidst a blaze of publicity in 1998, I was hugely disappointed, but not terribly surprised, when Haughey refused to be drawn into the controversy. This was one occasion when he could have repaid Veronica for all she had done for him, but when the opportunity arose, because of the difficulties he himself was facing he was unable to help.

Haughey's actions at the time of Veronica's death, and his failure to come out in support of her when Emily's book was published, surprised many people who had always felt that he was loyal to those who served him. Many of those who admired Haughey were not concerned at the revelations at the tribunals detailing the various payments he received – this was viewed as a separate matter. I too could understand his actions when faced with hard questions from tribunal lawyers – desperate men do desperate things. I still believe, however, that despite the difficulties he faced, he could have put the record straight. There is no doubt that Haughey's intervention at this time would have eased the pain of those close to Veronica.

***

Veronica's period of time working on the New Ireland Forum was a great personal success. She established many contacts and made many new friends. Her charisma resulted in her standing out from her peers and she enjoyed this period in her life a lot. Unlike a lot of backroom political workers, Veronica was not impressed by political leaders just because of who they were. Instead they had to gain her respect as she did theirs. She had an amazing ability to get along with all people, whether they were heads of state or football supporters whom she met on the terraces.

Veronica saw that there was a life outside of politics and that staying in the political system could only work if she stood for office. This did not interest her at all, so when the New Ireland Forum ended, she decided to move on. It had been indicated to her that she could remain in the employment of the Fianna Fáil Party, but this did not appeal to her.

Because of her involvement in politics, Veronica became interested in public relations and in 1998 started a business called Guerin Public Relations. This venture lasted about twelve months and was not a success. When the opportunity came up of a position in Club Air, a small airline that was founded by Club Travel boss Liam Lonnegan, Veronica jumped at it.

It was while working in the airline business that Veronica came across her first big story. In 1992 she approached the then editor of *The Sunday Business Post*, Damien Kiberd, asking for work. Her first story was on Aircraft Leasing Companies and others soon followed. Veronica wrote a number of high-profile stories for *The Sunday Business Post*, including pieces on the disappearance of IR£25 million from the Goodman Group and the Aer Lingus Holiday Homes disaster.

Veronica succeeded in breaking new ground and was soon noticed by other journalists who, even that early in her career, were extremely jealous of her contacts. They made the mistake, however, of believing that she would not last and that her stories would dry up. Veronica went about her business knowing that others were hoping for her to fail. She was bitterly disappointed when, in a court case with Aer Rianta, *The Sunday Business Post* accepted allegations that she had forged letters to secure PR work from a small airline company. Although they failed to back her in court, she continued to write for the paper following this incident.

It was at *The Sunday Business Post* that Veronica investigated her first crime story. It was about a well-known crime figure, Michael Travers, who had been shot in Darndale in north Dublin. She was asked to look at this story by her editor, who says that Veronica was delighted to be given the task. What her editor did not know was that Veronica already knew of Travers and a number of his associates, therefore this was an easy task for her. She produced a full-page story for the paper, and it was the reaction to this that developed her interest in crime. Veronica realised that, although people like to hear about business and politics, there is always a fascination with crime and criminals.

Veronica saw her time at *The Sunday Business Post* as an opportunity to start a new career. She was badly paid while working there, and her editor accepts that sometimes the money she received would not even have covered her travel expenses on a job. However, Veronica was not as interested in the income as she was in the opportunity that writing for a Sunday paper provided. It was a good arrangement and suited both parties. Veronica's time at the paper allowed her to establish a name for herself and brought her to the attention of other editors. She was soon approached by the *Sunday Tribune* and went to work for them.

Veronica joined the *Sunday Tribune* in the spring of 1993. This was a good career move and she was starting to receive proper money for her work, but, as always, this was not a driving factor. Alan Byrne, who was her editor, says that she never claimed expenses.

While Veronica was at the *Tribune*, the paper became more and more dependent upon her for lead stories. Week in and week out she was producing the best story of the week, and other journalists who were working there started to get jealous of her achievements. Veronica was not an exceptionally better journalist than her colleagues; the difference was that she worked harder. She got her results by calling to people connected to stories while others preferred to stay in an office and phone them. Veronica would sit outside someone's house waiting to get an interview while her colleagues were in the pub moaning that they could not get stories. She brought to journalism a work ethic that most of her colleagues could not comprehend. When her methods worked, and she became more successful, colleagues began to question Veronica's modus operandi and claimed she was irrational. Of course she made mistakes early on in her career, but so what? In their own words, the paper paid her peanuts, and, as her colleague at the *Sunday Independent* Rory Godson says, she lost her bad habits and grew more accomplished when she later moved to the *Independent*.

While at the *Tribune*, Veronica got a number of scoops. When Grace Livingstone was brutally murdered and her husband, who was one of the most senior tax inspectors in the country, was being treated as the prime suspect, Veronica got the first interview with him. She also broke the story about the use of funds in Tara Mines for political purposes.

While working with the *Sunday Tribune*, Veronica also established contacts in the criminal world. It was while doing this that she met Niall Mulvihill, who became one of her regular sources. Mulvihill, a bit of a fixer in the underworld in that he solved rows between various criminals and sorted out various disputes that arose between gang members, was one of the criminals involved in the theft of the Beit paintings. [1]

Mulvihill was shot dead in Dublin on 23 January, 2003, just two days after I had met with him as he was assisting with a story. He was passionate about football and loved everything about the

---

1. A collection of paintings owned by the collector Alfred Beit were stolen by a criminal gang from Russborough House in 1986.

game, and it was this that he had in common with Veronica. I met him many times after her death and I know he trusted, admired and respected her.

Their friendship was well known in both Garda and journalistic circles and it was this that enabled a reporter to claim that Mulvihill had told him that Veronica had asked him to supply her with a gun shortly before an incident in her home when she was shot in the leg. This claim was written within days of Mulvihill's death. Soon after, I wrote a piece about the reporter, Frank Connolly of *Ireland on Sunday*, who wrote the article. I knew Mulvihill well, and strongly believe that he would not have made such false claims about Veronica. I feel sorry for a reporter who snipes about the dead in order to settle scores with the living. I know that Frank Connolly was extremely annoyed at the fact that I had written a piece about his travelling to Columbia on a false passport and that he was questioned at Raheny Garda station concerning this. It is a sad way to seek revenge, speaking ill about those who are dead and have no chance to defend themselves, for the purposes of defaming their reputation and hurting those close to them.

On many occasions Niall Mulvihill told me stories about different journalists and politicians, including Frank Connolly. I often tried to confirm these stories, but as I could not, I didn't write about them. Other journalists obviously do not apply the same standards to their work.

Veronica's most notable scoop at the *Sunday Tribune* was the Bishop Casey interviews, which she secured in November 1993. Bishop Casey was one of the most senior figures within the Irish Catholic hierarchy. It had emerged that, while a much younger Bishop, he had fathered a child with a woman called Annie Murphy. When the story broke, Veronica made enquiries in an effort to establish the whereabouts of Bishop Casey, and from reliable contacts she discovered that he was in a small village in

Ecuador. Typical of her style, and at her own expense, Veronica travelled to Ecuador to deliver a letter to a colleague of the Bishop's in the hope of meeting with him. She struck lucky as, unknown to her, Bishop Casey was staying at the same house as his colleague.

Later that week, Veronica met Bishop Casey, and after spending many hours with him and using all her people skills, she convinced him to do a series of interviews with her. Many times he would lose his nerve and change his mind. He later told people that it was only because of Veronica and her manner that he agreed to do the interviews at all. This scoop proved to be a major success and it resulted in a huge increase in sales for the *Sunday Tribune*. Yet Veronica always spoke bitterly about how she was treated, both personally and financially, by the paper following these interviews.

She travelled half way around the world to get the Casey interviews, but her paper let her down badly when it came to rewarding her. She believed that her editor, Vincent Browne, now one of Ireland's best-known print and broadcast journalists, felt she was becoming too successful and that he resented this. He had tried to muscle his way into the interviews, but this had been rejected, not only by Veronica, but also by Bishop Casey, who said that he would do the interviews with Veronica and Veronica alone.

The *Sunday Tribune* had in Veronica a journalist who had secured stories that increased the circulation of the paper, but in 1994 they lost her to Ireland's largest selling newspaper, the *Sunday Independent*.

There is no doubt that the move to the *Sunday Independent* was a big step for Veronica. The paper's editor, Angus Fanning, recognised in her the potential to become the best reporter in the country. He had watched with envy as she produced sensational scoops for his competitors. Fanning was undoubtedly the most successful editor in the country at that time, and under his leadership, the *Sunday Independent* was going from strength to strength. Now he had landed one of the country's top reporters and her arrival would prove to be an unprecedented success. Fanning's number one concern was increasing the dominant position his paper enjoyed in the market place. The move also suited Veronica, who now had a platform that would allow her to continue to break award-winning and sensational stories.

It was this platform that would ultimately lead to Veronica's death, however, when she began to focus on crime stories. Soon after her arrival in the *Independent* offices on Abbey Street in 1994, Veronica broke the story about the delay in the Attorney General's office in dealing with the extradition of Father Brendan Smyth, who was accused of sexually abusing a number of children. This story was responsible for the break up of the Fianna Fáil/Labour Government, and led to the eventual downfall of Albert Reynolds as Taoiseach. However, Veronica was encouraged to concentrate on crime. She soon became one of the most popular contributors to the paper as she introduced the readers to a world that was previously unknown to them, yet was on their doorstep.

***

As Veronica worked to expose the criminals and their gangs, she herself was becoming more and more exposed. The truth is that she was writing about the most dangerous people in our society, but she was alone. Her copy was submitted and then sensationalised, the more dramatic the headline, the more papers would be sold. She was becoming more and more famous and the sales at the *Sunday Independent* were reaching unprecedented levels. Like a good centre-forward, to remain at the top you need to keep scoring, and there was competitiveness among her crime colleagues in other papers. The *Sunday Independent* needed her to remain on top, and this was encouraged in the material that she was allowed to write.

It was one of these pieces on crime that led to the first serious attack on Veronica. One evening in October 1994, shots were fired through the window of her home. This was a clear attempt to intimidate her. However, little changed and Veronica kept reporting. Week after week she wrote about criminals and their activities. The criminals were now being given nicknames and her readership grew and grew. Marketing took hold and Veronica's contribution to the paper's success was now becoming obvious as she appeared more frequently in advertising campaigns. Constant radio and television appearances resulted in her becoming Ireland's most recognisable journalist. By now she was in danger, not only from criminals whom she wrote about who feared her work, but also from colleagues who envied her success.

It was at this time that Veronica wrote articles about the personal life of Martin Cahill aka 'The General'. An informant, John Traynor, had given Veronica information on Cahill and other criminals. Traynor, who was a well-known criminal himself, was one of Veronica's main sources.

Traynor had given Veronica details about the unusual relationship that existed between Martin Cahill, his wife and her sister. When this story ran, Cahill was furious and let it be known that he was aware that it had been Traynor who had given Veronica this information about his private life. Traynor knew that not only was he in trouble with Cahill, but he was also in danger of losing out financially as it was being said that he could no longer be trusted. Little did his criminal friends realise that Traynor wasn't just supplying Veronica with information about their activities, he was also one of senior Gardaí's best touts.

Traynor realised that his situation was becoming desperate. He stood to lose everything if he could not make amends with the crime bosses that he depended on for his millions. He was also fearful that Cahill would have him dealt with if the situation continued. He decided that he would have to take decisive action and arranged for Veronica to be attacked again at her home.

In January 1995, a gunman called to Veronica's home and shot her in the leg. It is still unclear if this was a warning or an attempt to silence her. This was the second gun attack on Veronica as a result of her investigative journalism into the criminal underworld.

After Veronica's murder in 1996, Charles Bowden, who had been involved in the murder, claimed in his testimony to Gardaí that it was John Traynor who had set Veronica up on the day that she was murdered. Veronica had made the error of telling Traynor when she had to appear in court on speeding charges, and he had passed this information to the criminal gang who used the opportunity to kill her.

Traynor was one of Veronica's main criminal underworld sources, but even though it is known that he provided the information that led to her eventual murder, he has never been arrested for his part in this crime. He now continues to distribute drugs in this country from his base in the south of Spain. Although he was arrested by the Dutch authorities after Veronica's murder, along with another criminal, Brian Meehan, he was subsequently released as there was no warrant out for his arrest.

It was after the second attack on Veronica's home that, in my view, her employers began to fail her. It was clear at that stage that her life was in serious danger and more could have and should have been done to protect her. It is easy for the *Sunday Independent* to say, as they have on many occasions, that they installed an alarm at her home. Quite simply this was not enough. They say that she was offered the chance to write about other topics, but experience has shown me that nothing matters more to the *Sunday Independent* than sales. I do not believe that she was encouraged to write about different topics as these would not have had the same appeal to the public as her work on crime. The *Sunday Independent* was selling more papers than ever before. It is a company run by many people who all share a goal. That goal is to sell papers. I am not suggesting for one moment that any individual decided that Veronica's life was worth an increase in sales, but I firmly believe that when decisions were being made, the priority was the interests of the paper rather than the journalist. Another crime journalist, Paul Williams, who was working in the *Sunday World*, a sister paper of the Independent group, was often provided with protection and minders.

The Gardaí placed protection on Veronica for a number of weeks after she was shot in the leg in January 1995, but when Veronica asked the Gardaí to withdraw their protection, the paper never replaced this or made any other arrangements to ensure her safety. She decided that she could no longer work effectively with Garda minders travelling behind her. If the Gardaí were concerned enough to give Veronica protection, then the *Independent* should have realised that Veronica needed some assistance.

There was no cooling off period after this second attack, and soon Veronica was back to reporting serious crime. It was at this point, unknown to herself and, in fairness, to her employers, that she was about to start investigating one of the country's most dangerous criminals. Veronica started to look into the affairs of John Gilligan, a criminal who in a few short years after being released from prison was worth many millions of pounds.

***

John Gilligan was released from Portlaoise prison in 1993, where he had been serving a sentence for handling stolen property. In the space of three years, he became one of the biggest drug dealers in the history of the state.

On 7 September, 1995, Veronica wrote to John Gilligan to inform him that she was writing an article, which would include reference to him and his newfound wealth. She received no reply. One week later, she called to his home at his equestrian centre in Enfield, Co. Kildare. Veronica was brutally assaulted by John

Gilligan when she visited his home that day. She later went to her local police station and made the following statement recalling the events.

'I arrived at the equestrian centre at approximately 8.50 am. The centre was open and I spoke to a lady who appeared to be the administrator. I asked to speak with Mr Gilligan and was told that he was not there, but that I could find him at the private home adjacent to the centre. This lady explained to me how best to drive to that house. She told me I should use the intercom on the gate to the house to make contact with Mr Gilligan. I returned to my car and drove to the private house as directed. I stopped at the electrified gates at the front of his house.

'I got out of my car and walked over to the intercom. I pressed the intercom switch a number of times and announced my presence. I noticed the presence of surveillance cameras in the area of the electrified gates and I stood in a position which I believe ensured that I was clearly visible to the occupant of the house.

'After a short period of time, the electrified gates at the entrance to the residence opened. I waited for a moment to see if any person or a car was coming out. No car came out and there was nobody there. I realised that I was being admitted onto the grounds of this residence. I travelled up the length of the driveway and parked my car beside the entrance to the house. I noticed Mr Gilligan's Land Rover Jeep parked outside the house.

'I got out of my car and went over to the door and knocked at the door of the house using the door knocker. I saw surveillance cameras scanning the door area and I stood in a position which I believe ensured that I was clearly visible to the occupant of the house. The door opened and I saw Mr Gilligan dressed in a silk dressing gown. Mr Gilligan said, 'Yeah?' I then said, 'Mr Gilligan?' and he said, 'That's right.' I introduced myself and explained to him that I wanted to ask him some questions. As I spoke I noticed he became very agitated and then I took a step back.

'Mr Gilligan then suddenly, and without warning, came out of the doorway and grabbed me violently about the upper part of my body. He struck me violently about the head and face with his fists. He shouted at me that if I wrote one word about him he would, "fucking kill you, your husband, your fucking son, your family, everybody belonging to you, even your fucking neighbours".

'Mr Gilligan seemed to be carrying me to my car. He continued to hit me in the area of my head, face and upper part of my body with his fists. He pushed me onto the bonnet of my car and continued to beat me about the head and face with his fists. He released me from his grip and allowed me slide to the ground. He said, "Get the fuck out of here. Get off my fucking property." As I opened the door he grabbed me and pushed me into the car. He continued to threaten that he would harm both my family and myself if I wrote anything about him. As I tried to start my car he leaned in and said "Have you a fucking mike? Where is the fucking wire?" I replied, "No, I have nothing."'

Gilligan then ripped open Veronica's shirt to ensure there was no wire and continued to make threats against her and her family. As she left his home, she was in pain and shock. She immediately headed to her mother's house and then to her doctor. At 1.05 pm that same day, Gilligan called her on his mobile phone. He explained that all the property was in his wife's name and that they were legally separated. Then he said, 'If you [write] one thing on me, or write about me, I am going to kidnap your son and ride him. I am going to shoot you. Do you understand what I am saying to you? I am going to kidnap your fucking son and ride him. I am going to shoot you; I am going to fucking kill you.'

This incident caused a lot of concern for people close to Veronica. People were worried that she was going too far, but everyone supported her decision to press charges against Gilligan for the assault. However, while the *Sunday Independent* was well aware of Gilligan's threats to her, she remained without protection.

Veronica was a sitting target and the potential danger she was in caused great concern for her family. My wife Louann was very distressed when she read of the incidents and took the threats very seriously. She was worried that if Veronica continued to write about Gilligan then our children could be at risk. We had reason to be worried; we were the only Guerin siblings in the phone book at that time. The whole situation was causing us so much concern that we sought legal advice to see if we could prevent articles being published that placed us in danger. The legal advice we received was that there was nothing we could do. I also spoke to Veronica who dismissed my concerns out of hand.

The *Sunday Independent* could have acted. They could have insisted that Veronica accept the Garda protection offered. If Veronica did not want Garda protection, then they could have provided her with minders who would not have inhibited her continuing with her work. Instead they reported each incident to the fullest so that papers would sell. Their attitude was that that was their job, let Veronica do hers.

Veronica proceeded with the charges against Gilligan and took the case of assault all the way. On 25 June 1996, Veronica appeared in Kilcock courthouse to face John Gilligan. The case was adjourned and Gilligan headed for the airport. He was leaving the country as he did not want to be around the following day.

***

One of the worst murders in the history of the state and certainly in my lifetime .... It took a journalist to shock us all into seeing what we are up against.

An Taoiseach, Bertie Ahern, 26 June, 1996

Wednesday, 26 June, 1996, was a bright summer's day. Veronica was up early to get Cathal ready and then herself dressed for work.

Her mind was preoccupied with her appearance in Naas District Court later that morning. She had every right to worry. This would not be first time that Veronica had faced speeding charges. She knew that if she lost her driving licence she would be unable to carry on with her work. No doubt she was speeding even as she drove to Naas courthouse that day.

As Veronica was leaving her home in Cloghran, north Dublin, Brian Meehan, Gilligan's second-in-command in his profitable drug operation, was heading for a lock-up garage in Terenure where he had arranged to collect a stolen high-powered motorbike from one of Gilligan's bagmen, Russell Warren. Warren's job in the Gilligan gang was to collect the money, have it counted and batched, and then deliver it to various exchange offices in Belgium and Holland. On 26 June, 1996, Warren was due to go to Holland to change and launder more of Gilligan's drug money. However, the previous day he had been told by Meehan that Gilligan wanted him to stay in Dublin. Meehan offered Warren no explanation at the time. Warren was told to be at the lock-up garage in Terenure the next morning where Meehan would collect the stolen bike from him.

Warren would later claim in court that this was all he knew. The following morning, Meehan arrived shortly before 10 am to collect the bike and Warren met him as arranged. Meehan told Warren that John Gilligan wanted him (Warren) to go to Naas to follow a red Opel Calibra car. Meehan also gave him a description of a woman and told him that her name was Veronica Guerin. Warren was then told that she would be at the courthouse, and that when he spotted the car, he was to contact Meehan on his mobile phone. He was to also phone Gilligan and keep him posted about what was happening.

Just as Meehan drove off, Warren got a call from Gilligan, who instructed him to do as Meehan had said and keep in contact with Meehan and himself at all times. It was early, so Warren went for breakfast around the corner from the garage. He then headed to

Naas. It took him over an hour to get there, and when he arrived, he mistook the local Social Welfare office for the courthouse. He then approached a uniformed Garda to ask for directions to the courthouse. Warren claimed later in court that the fact that he approached a Garda at this time confirms that he was totally unaware of what was going on. He maintained that had he known what he was involved in, he would never have spoken to the Garda, and run the risk of tying himself to one of the scenes related to a brutal murder.

As Warren was scouting the area in Naas, Meehan made the short journey to a warehouse in Greenmount Industrial Estate in Harold's Cross that was used as a distribution centre for the drug gang. Here he picked up a passenger and a .357 revolver.

Charlie Bowden, the quartermaster of the drugs gang and the man who looked after the huge cache of arms that Gilligan's gang had imported along with the drugs, had loaded the revolver the previous day. Peter Mitchell, who had used Bowden to courier drugs for him a few years earlier, introduced him to the Gilligan gang. Bowden had been in the army, where he had become an expert marksman. He was also a karate champion. He was considered perfect for the Gilligan drug operation, not least because he was unknown to Gardaí and could deliver drugs around the city unnoticed.

Meehan and his passenger then headed in the direction of the Naas Road, where they awaited notification from Warren that he had spotted Veronica.

Veronica was in good form as she emerged from the courthouse. She had escaped with a warning and a fine of IR£150. Delighted with her good luck, she returned to her car and started to call people on her mobile phone to share her good news. A huge weight had been lifted from her shoulders as she still had her driving licence, one of the vital tools of her trade.

Warren went to the courthouse and looked for Veronica and the car. Failing to see either, he went around the corner and bought a paper and a mineral. It was while he was walking back to the courthouse that he saw Veronica driving away in her car. He phoned Meehan and told him that he had seen Veronica, and that she was leaving Naas. Meehan instructed him to follow the car and to keep in touch with him at all times.

As she made her way under the bridge at Naas and headed for the dual carriageway, Veronica failed to notice that she was being followed. Warren, who was driving a blue Lite Ace van, had caught up and was now only a few cars behind her. Again he spoke to Meehan and confirmed Veronica's location, sending her to her death.

By now, Meehan and the gunman were waiting on a motorbike at a lay-by off the Naas Road, just outside the Airmotive plant. As Veronica approached, they spotted her car and pulled out and followed it. Warren saw them following Veronica, both wearing full visors. Veronica was unaware of what was happening and continued to use her mobile phone, calling people to give them her good news.

As Veronica approached the Boot Road junction, the lights turned red, and she stopped in traffic, three cars from the lights. As she did, Meehan and the gunman pulled up alongside her. The gunman casually dismounted from the bike. He walked to the car and drew a gun from inside his jacket. As he approached Veronica, she was phoning a garda friend to tell him her good news. This friend had been slagging her that she would lose her licence and she wanted to let him know how wrong he was. This banter between friends was Veronica at her best. Disappointed that her friend was not answering, Veronica started to leave a message on his mobile phone. She had just spoken a few words when suddenly the window smashed, and the gunman fired six bullets into her at point blank range.

The first shot hit Veronica in the neck and she raised her arm in order to protect herself. She leaned across the car as if attempting to escape through the passenger door when he fired a further five shots into her back. The post-mortem revealed that there were injuries to Veronica's index fingers where she tried helplessly to protect herself from the firing bullets. It is known that Veronica did not die instantly as she was able to attempt an escape, but the bullets entered both of her lungs and an artery, and she died in a matter of minutes.

Various reports about Veronica's last moments have been written. In one of these, a journalist suggested that Veronica pleaded with her killer not to shoot her in the face. This same colleague went on American television and claimed that Veronica's last words had been, 'Not in the face'. This made good copy, but was totally untrue. It also left those close to Veronica wondering if she had in fact died quickly or if she had suffered. This claim led us to believe that Veronica had been aware of what was happening and had suffered before she died. However, this was not in fact the case. It materialised that the story had come from Meehan, who had told this lie in a pub the night Veronica was murdered. Meehan, is said to have relayed this version in the Hole In the Wall pub as he and his gang celebrated Veronica's death.

A couple who were parked two cars ahead and to the side of Veronica's car heard the shots. They went to her assistance and saw her body slumped over the seat. The man in the car, Brian McNamara, had initially thought that the noise was a car backfiring, but when he looked around, he saw what appeared to be a man shooting into a car and then putting his hand back into his leather jacket before getting back on a motorbike. Mr McNamara then saw the motorbike coming toward them and turning off the dual carriageway.

A few cars behind, Nurse Brenda Grogan was sitting in her car with her radio playing loudly. She was on her way to work in the Mater Hospital. When she realised that the traffic was not moving even though the lights had changed, she assumed something was wrong. A few moments later, thinking that a driver must have taken ill, she walked from her car to the traffic lights, where she saw Veronica's car. Brenda noticed that a woman was slumped across the front seats and that the man who had been trying to help her was covered in blood. She rushed to the car and felt for a pulse in Veronica's neck, but she could not find one, she tried again, but there was no sign of life.

A woman who had been trained in midwifery assisted her, and Brian McNamara, who was very upset, insisted they should try and do something. As they lifted Veronica into an upright position, her head fell back. Brenda placed her ear close to Veronica's face to see if she could feel her breathing, but there was no breath. It was then she noticed the gaping wound in Veronica's neck and realised that Veronica was dead.

***

Russell Warren claims that it was only at this stage that he realised exactly what was happening. He says that he was shocked and his stomach was churning, and that he just wanted to get out of there. He recalled in court, 'I realised what I was after doing, after helping to murder somebody.' However, these words seem hollow when considered alongside his actions. The truth is that Warren played a major part in killing Veronica. The bike he had stolen one month previously and had handed over to Veronica's killers earlier that day had been used in a savage cold-blooded murder.

After the shooting, Warren immediately escaped from the scene of the crime by driving off the dual carriageway and up a slip road into Clondalkin before going onto on the M50. Here he stopped and phoned Gilligan, relaying to him what had happened. Gilligan asked if they had gotten away and if Veronica was dead. He then warned Warren that this is what would happen to him if he ever made a statement against his boss.

Although he later claimed that he was immediately full of remorse, Warren headed home where he changed his clothes. He then met friends and went with them for a drink in Rathgar. He lent the van that he had used to follow Veronica and monitor her movements for her killers to a friend, and then he placed bets in the afternoon before watching a football match in a pub that evening. While he was in the pub, Warren heard people discuss the killing and also saw reports on the television. He has since admitted that nothing in his behaviour would have indicated that he had just been involved in this brutal killing. This, in my view, shows the real Warren, a cold-blooded murderer who displayed no remorse after being involved in the slaying of a young mother. Warren eventually turned state's evidence so that he could avoid prosecution for his role in Veronica's murder. He did this, not because he felt remorse, but because he saw it as a better deal for himself, and how right he was.

***

Meehan and the killer escaped from the scene, cleaned up and got rid of the weapon and the bike. They then went about the business of creating alibis for themselves.

Gilligan was in his hotel suite in Amsterdam with his young mistress, celebrating what he believed to be the end of his troubles. He contacted Meehan when he learned of the killing from Warren, and congratulated him on his success. Meehan made his way to the centre of town and spoke with his accomplice Charlie Bowden. Both wanted to be seen, so they met and talked on the road instead of at Bowden's premises or a coffee shop.

That night, Gilligan's gang celebrated in the Hole in the Wall pub near the Phoenix Park. They joked about the murder they had carried out earlier that day. They bragged about how cool the assassin had been, and how Gilligan was pleased. They really believed that a good day's work had been done. The gang soon had to leave the pub, however, because Meehan got into a fight in the toilets. Later that night they all returned to Bowden's house at the Paddocks on the Navan Road, where they had a party which went on late into the evening.

Bowden's house was later burned to the ground when Bowden turned state's evidence, which he did in an attempt to avoid prosecution for his major part in a brutal murder. Like Warren, Bowden claimed that he wanted to give evidence because he felt remorse. I firmly believe, however, after watching all his appearances in court, that he felt no remorse for what he did and only turned evidence in an attempt at damage limitation on his part. This was a decision that has no doubt paid dividends for Bowden.

***

It's unnatural for a mother to bury her young.

As I drove through town I tried to figure out how I would face the task before me without Veronica. When I had to tell my mother that my father had died, Veronica had helped me, we planned what I should say to my mother and then who we should call. This time Veronica could not help because it was Veronica who was dead. She was more than a sister to me, she was a friend and someone I could rely on when faced with a difficult situation. Veronica was gone and I was left to face this painful task alone.

It was one o'clock in the afternoon on Wednesday, 26 June, 1996, when I received a call from my friend Sean Paul. He asked if I had heard that Veronica had been shot. I replied that I had not; he said he thought it was true and he would find out more. I could tell from his voice that he was upset, and thought to myself, 'Not again, I hope she is okay.' I thought that maybe Sean Paul was mistaken as I had not heard this news from anyone else and none of my family had been on to me.

A few moments later the phone rang again, this time Sean Paul was more upset and sounded as if he was crying. I knew straight away that it was bad news, but I never imagined that Veronica was dead. Sean Paul said he had confirmed with a friend of his in the newsroom of the radio station 98FM that Veronica had been shot and he thought it was bad.

I just sat motionless as I put down the phone, and seconds later it rang again. This time it was my mother's sister and she confirmed my worst thoughts. Veronica had been shot dead on the Naas Road. My aunt remained calm as she explained to me what had happened. She was anxious that I locate my mother and tell her the news.

As I walked slowly to my car my hands shook and I felt sick; I could not believe what had happened. My thoughts were with my mother, as I knew that she would never get over this. I pictured Mam smiling somewhere, chatting happily to friends, not knowing that her youngest daughter lay dead on the Naas Road. Tears filled my eyes as I prayed that Veronica had not suffered. The phone kept ringing. Where was Mam? Who would tell her? Everyone was in shock, with people crying as we discussed what had happened. Everyone asked where Mam was, we had to get to her.

My aunt called again and told me that my mother was attending a doctor in Beaumont Hospital, and I would find her there. The family had agreed that it would be me who would break this awful news to my mother.

I phoned my wife Louann, who was at home with our children. I told her that Veronica had been shot and that I thought she was dead. Louann was devastated. By the time I called her back some moments later, neighbours had already begun to call to her. That was very frightening, people outside the family had begun to hear the awful news. It was vital that I locate my mother and tell her as I did not want her reading about it or hearing it from a stranger as she went about her day.

My aunt called again, this time she was more specific and explained to me that Mam had an appointment with a specialist in Beaumont private clinic. I headed straight there and asked at reception if I could speak with Mrs Guerin. The lady checked and said that there was no record of her appointment. I tried to remain calm; I insisted that there must be an error and asked if she would check again. The reception area was crowded and I fought back the tears and made small talk as I waited for my mother to appear.

I then received another call from my aunt who informed me that my mother's appointment was in fact in the consultant's surgery on Landsdowne Road, which was on the opposite side of town. I thanked the receptionist, apologised for my error, headed for my car and started what seemed an endless journey to town.

As soon as I got to my car I again phoned Louann to bring her up to date with what was happening. I was relieved that a friend of ours, Ray Robinson, who is calm and very capable in an emergency, was with Louann. Both her sisters had arrived and were helping her with our children so I knew she was being well looked after. Louann told me that my sister, Marie Therese, who lived just a few hundred yards away, had called. She had been round to my mother's house, but there was no one there. Marie Therese, who was in a state of shock and upset, then left our house to gather up her own family and find out exactly what had happened.

My sister Claire was in Cork on holidays with her husband. Senior staff at the hotel where they were staying had been advised of Veronica's death and were going to tell Claire's husband when they arrived so he could relay the news. My brother Martin, the eldest, was on his way to the scene of the shooting.

Following my mother's appointment with her consultant, she was due to meet one of her sisters and her brother-in-law for afternoon tea. They had been told what had happened and had gone straight to my mother at the consultant's rooms, but they did not tell her the news. While awaiting my arrival, they spun my mother a line that her files had to be brought from Beaumont over to her consultant's surgery on Lansdowne Road. When she was brought to his private sitting room she chatted away to her sister, oblivious to what was happening. The scene was set for me to arrive and tell her this terrible news.

As I parked my car on Lansdowne Road, I recalled again how difficult it had been 13 years earlier telling my mother that my father had died. Recalling her reaction that day, I was shaking at the prospect of telling her about Veronica. I have never before felt so helpless and alone. The sun was shining, but I was close to tears as I made my way down the narrow path leading to the hall door. I thought I could not face this task, could not break this news to my mother, and found myself walking away. Yet I realised that it had to be done, it had to be done by one of her children and I had been chosen to do it. I made my way back to the door and knocked.

As I waited for the door to be answered, I recalled the many times I had heard my mother say, 'It's unnatural for a mother to bury her young.' Now I would have to tell her that her greatest fear had been realised. On the previous occasion that Veronica had been shot, I had to break the news to my mother and my brother Martin, and bring them to the hospital. This time there would be no visiting Veronica and no chance to hold her. This time there would be no point in questioning Veronica about what she was doing.

The staff in the consultant's surgery greeted me kindly and led me to where my mother was. I could hear her talking to her sister and I thought to myself that my aunt was being unbelievably strong for my mother's sake. They were making a daunting task somewhat easier for me just by being there. As I stepped up the small flight of stairs to the room I went cold and a shiver ran through my body. My mother was seated on a large sofa; she turned and greeted me with her warm smile as always. Then she asked, 'What are you doing here?' As she did, I sat beside her and held her hand. My aunt and her husband had walked to the window of the large room and were staring straight out. I could see they were both crying. I just held Mam's hand and said, 'Veronica has been involved in another shooting.' I don't know where I got the strength to continue. The blood drained from my mother's face, she said, 'No, how is she?' I looked at her and said, 'Veronica is dead.'

My mother's reaction was frightening as it was one of total disbelief. She refused to listen and could not accept what I was saying. Her sister came and comforted her with me. Her doctor gave her some medication to relax her, and after tea and tears we headed for my mother's home. She travelled with her sister. As I walked to my car, I cried and prayed that never again would I have to tell someone that they had lost a child.

As I headed back across the city alone, I called Louann, who had made arrangements for our children to go to their cousins'. I arranged to meet her in my mother's house and she was heading there as we spoke. Suddenly I realised that never again would I see Veronica alive. No more laughs or fights, and there had been plenty of both. No more Veronica, but how could I accept that? How could any of our family accept that? We were close as a family unit, closer than most families that I knew. But death brings many things and a loss has many consequences. One of the consequences of Veronica's loss was that, as a family, we would never be as united again. Veronica's murderers not only killed Veronica, but also took the reason for living from my mother and destroyed what was a close family unit.

***

There was a year and 13 days between Veronica and myself. We always palled around in the same groups; either she tagged with me or vice versa. Veronica had a passion for sport and always loved to compete. From an early age she would be as good, if not better, than most of the local boys at football, and it used to give me great pride to see her being one of the first picked when teams were being put together for games of football on the green outside our house. This love of sport was probably what contributed most to her personality. She always went the extra yard, never shirked from a tackle and was a team player.

I remember when a local priest, Fr Casey, formed the basketball club that was to become a major part of Veronica's life. She joined a team, Killester Kittens, the original Killester ladies team and probably its best ever. They won most of the basketball competitions that they entered. The girls from that team were all students in St Mary's in Killester, and their school team went on to win the European championships. Veronica sustained a back injury playing basketball, and I often watched her play through a game in great pain rather than let her side down. She was one of a number of outstanding players on that team and played for her country numerous times.

It was not only at basketball that Veronica excelled. The fact that she was a tomboy when growing up paid dividends, and Veronica played international football for Ireland. One of her team-mates was Irish international Frank Stapleton's sister Helena, herself a gifted player and probably Veronica's closest friend. Helena was one of Veronica's bridesmaids, and I always remember how much fun she was on Veronica's wedding day. That Veronica had chosen me to give her away made it one of the proudest days in my life. I know that no one could replace the love Veronica had for our father, but that she let me take his place that day was something I will always cherish.

Growing up, Veronica had a bubbly personality. She was a leader rather than a follower. Many neighbours who watched her play football and do things as well as the lads would have regarded her as wild. She also took chances. She would mitch from school and sneak into dances in town. She was wild in that sense of the word. She was also extremely clever and did well in exams at all levels. When we would not be allowed out till our homework was completed, Veronica would finish mine. While always a tomboy, she was an extremely attractive girl and stood out among her peers with her good looks. She was streetwise and knew what was regarded as cool. Veronica was a great friend as well as a sister. This meant I could talk to her about anything and we gave each other advice from our gender's point of view.

When I was driving back to my mother's house from Ballsbridge, I realised that I would never share these talks with her again.

***

We eventually arrived at what was to be our base for the next three days. My mother was numb as she walked into our home. Soon neighbours and friends were calling to express their sympathy, but I was walking around in a daze as people expressed their sorrow. Everyone who called was crying, and I remember that I could not understand why I had not cried properly yet. On reflection it was because I kept myself busy. Louann arrived and as always gave me great strength. She had taken care of our three young children, and then looked after people as they arrived to my mother's. At this stage none of the other family members were at my mother's home. They were with Veronica's husband Graham at his house. My mother was in another world as people sympathised with her. We had heard that my sister Claire was on her way up from Cork.

During the afternoon, news flashes kept showing pictures of Veronica's car out at the Naas Road. It was difficult for us knowing that under the sheets that covered her car lay Veronica's body. This was a cause of great concern for our family, we knew it was no one's fault, but that did not ease our pain. It was difficult and upsetting for us to think of Veronica lying there. We did not know then how important it was for Gardaí to take their time and to collect all available evidence before removing the body of a victim. When Assistant Commissioner Pat O'Toole called to our home to sympathise with my mother, we explained our concerns and he acted promptly. Soon after, Veronica's remains were brought to Blanchardstown Hospital.

Later that night Cathal Cryan, a friend of Veronica's who was a detective sergeant, drove Graham, one of my brothers-in-law and myself to the hospital to identify Veronica's body. This was an awful experience. We were not allowed in for some hours and had to go away and come back. To see Veronica laid out and being looked at this way by strangers was a most upsetting experience. We all said our goodbyes, but then as we were leaving the morgue, Dr Harbison called after Graham and requested that he formally identify Veronica's body. I felt so sorry for Graham as he had to clearly say, 'Yes, this is the body of my wife.'

As a family we were not allowed the time to grieve, something that, in many ways, was denied to us until Gilligan was jailed. The evening of Veronica's murder seemed endless. When we returned from identifying her body, there were more people in the house, more drinks to pour and more tea to make. Everyone was so kind. More and more it was beginning to sink in that Veronica was dead.

I regret not being able to appreciate the tributes to Veronica that were made at that time by people from all walks of life. The tributes that were paid in the Dáil and elsewhere are a great honour for her. Veronica would have laughed at some of those who were speaking of her bravery and her contribution to Irish life.

At this stage we had to prepare for the funeral, which to my surprise would leave from my mother's house and not from Veronica's home. This had not been planned, it just seemed to happen. The day following Veronica's murder was spent getting organised, sorting out where the children would be, who would bring them to the removal and so on. It also allowed us some time to be alone with our spouses. That time with Louann was important to me. It allowed me to be myself and not feel that I had to be doing the 'right thing'. We made arrangements for our own children and then we met with a few friends who were part of the original Ógra Fianna Fáil circle. This group was made up of old friends who had shared many weekends away, plotted many elections and were so close, we had become like family.

We decided then that we would go and visit Veronica, and as we did, we reminisced and recalled the many incidents that happened down the years, the many places visited, the fights, the making up and the sheer fun that we had enjoyed. That night turned out to be one of the funniest and saddest Ógra Fianna Fáil meetings that was ever held. We laughed, cried, told stupid jokes, had serious discussions, and most of all we were ourselves with Veronica. It was a special time for all of us. I remember leaving the funeral home with tears coming down my face, tears of sadness and tears of laughter. We had just finished a very special evening and no one would have appreciated it more than Veronica herself. As we left, someone commented that Veronica had never been so quiet at an Ógra meeting before.

The following day we all went to the funeral home and I brought my mother down to see Veronica. A lot of people did not want her to go, but others, including Louann, felt she should. It was the right decision and one I know she is glad was made. Things were becoming tetchy in our home and it had come to a stage when it was wise for us to spend time away from one another.

The day after Veronica was murdered, Bertie Ahern and John O'Donoghue came to our home to see my mother. Louann recalls that the teapot in our house was damaged, and as she poured tea for Bertie, they both laughed as it leaked all over the floor and saucer. There is undoubted warmth about Ahern and it is his genuineness that people like. Ahern felt a special sadness and was deeply moved as he recounted to us that he had spent time with Veronica only two weeks earlier at the funeral of the late Detective

Gerry McCabe, who was also gunned down in cold blood by ruthless assassins.

Veronica was later moved from North Strand to Maypark in Donnycarney where the removal was held. We were to leave our home at 4.30 pm and the house filled with sympathisers. It was becoming more and more of a traditional wake. Sir Antony O'Reilly, who thought he would be late, arrived at our home and sympathised with us all. It was clear that he was genuinely shaken by Veronica's murder. He and his son Gavin shared our loss and were deeply moved. Again there was a light moment when we were getting up to go to the removal and my mother lifted the tray and handed it someone telling them to take it to the kitchen. She then turned to Sir Tony and told him to unplug the television before we left. As one would expect, he respectfully did as he was told.

When we arrived at the funeral home, I remember being totally taken aback by the large crowd that had gathered there. There were thousands of people and I was very moved that so many people from all walks of life had turned out to pay their respects to Veronica.

The prayers in Stafford's funeral home were comforting, and this difficult time was made easier as so many friends surrounded us. The journey to the airport church took no time as we had a Garda escort. It was clear from the removal that the church the next morning would be chaotic, and I was asked to assist the undertaker and the priest in identifying family and arranging seating.

Veronica's funeral mass was attended by President Robinson, the Taoiseach and most members of the Government, as well as all the leaders and prominent figures from all the political parties. Many ambassadors also attended and their seating had to be arranged. This was an onerous task, but with the help of people from the Taoiseach's department and others from Murray Consultants, the *Independent*'s public relation's firm, all went well. Before the mass, we met all the dignitaries and spoke with them.

President Robinson said that she did not know how we felt and hoped she never would. Her honesty was refreshing and highlighted the terrible loss we had just suffered.

In the aftermath of the funeral we tried to get on with our lives, but this proved next to impossible. I kept questioning if more could have been done to prevent this awful murder. I questioned my own part and asked if I had done enough, and if what I had done was in an effort to protect my own family or to protect Veronica. The truth is that not enough had been done, and had people been more concerned about Veronica's safety, she would be alive today.

I am in favour of a free press and I accept its importance in a democracy. But this importance places a huge responsibility on newspaper editors and proprietors everywhere. They must take all the necessary steps to provide the resources required to protect the journalists that supply us with that same free press that we all agree is so important.

***

Veronica's murder resulted in an unprecedented Garda investigation that would change gangland Dublin as any of us knew it. The biggest manhunt in the state was underway and there would be no hiding place for those responsible for Veronica's death.

On 25 July, 1996, one month after Veronica was murdered, legislation introducing the Proceeds of Crime Act, 1996, was moved in the Dáil. I was present in the visitors' gallery when John O'Donoghue moved the legislation. Fianna Fáil was in opposition at the time, but the rainbow coalition allowed the legislation and, with some amendments, it was passed. That was the beginning of a task force that was to become the envy of police forces across the world.

On 31 July, 1996, the Criminal Assets Bureau came into existence. It would no longer be possible for criminals to flaunt their wealth as the state now had the power to seize assets that could not be accounted for. No longer could a drug dealer decide to buy a house or car from the proceeds of his drug business. If someone could not explain the source of his or her assets then the state could seize these and the burden of proof was on the criminal. Since it was formed, hundreds of millions of euro have been gathered by the Bureau. Soon the biggest criminals in Ireland would be fleeing the country and establishing their bases elsewhere.

That night at the end of July I was in the bar in Leinster house and I was particularly sad. Fourteen years earlier I had participated in a debate for young Fianna Fáil. We had moved that the state take possession of the assets of the crime kings who were destroying our city. I had proposed that the people march on the home of the convicted drug baron Christy Dunne, who had a magnificent home in the Dublin Mountains, and turn it into a rehabilitation clinic. Had the warnings been heeded then would there be a Criminal Assets Bureau now, and far more importantly, would Veronica be alive today?

As the investigation into Veronica's murder proceeded, the media frenzy grew and slowly those colleagues who had it in for Veronica came out of the woodwork. Some did not wait long. It was only days before Vincent Browne said that she was a bad writer. In *The Sunday Times* he found a good playmate; that paper also wanted to attack Veronica so it could embarrass the *Sunday Independent* and maybe exploit this tragedy for commercial gain. I remember how it all began with subtle remarks in the newspapers and then a dreadful article appeared in *The Sunday Times* magazine, which was extremely critical about Veronica. This piece was written by Maeve Sheehan who is now employed at the *Sunday Independent*.

After that the floodgates opened. The biggest onslaught, which not surprisingly came from the Vincent Browne stable, was in the guise of a book written by the current ombudsman and former journalist Emily O'Reilly. Emily contacted me and was anxious to speak about the awful events that had happened surrounding Veronica. I was fortunate because Emily seemed to think that I believed all that she said. I enjoyed playing this role as it enabled me find out as much as possible about Emily's real agenda and what sort of story she wished to tell about Veronica.

Emily did herself proud the first day I met her. I had reluctantly agreed to meet with her in the Marine Hotel in Sutton, and she cried as she spoke about Veronica. I knew that this was an act. I had been told by former colleagues of Veronica's that Emily was allegedly one of those who spread rumours about Veronica when she was alive. I felt she would be no different now that Veronica was dead.

The book Emily eventually wrote about Veronica was not well received, but it did create hurt for those close to Veronica. She broke all the promises she had made, which did not surprise me; however, it did create difficulty for me with others, as I had asked her to contact my other siblings, which she had assured me she would do but did not. In my innocence, I had thought that any reporter would try to gather as much information about their subject as possible. In Emily's case this was not to be, one of the many things that separated her and others from Veronica.

Emily would contact me, saying, 'You know Veronica did this and that?' And when, with the generous help of others, I could prove beyond doubt that Emily was wrong, she would have to drop her scurrilous allegations. I always knew that when this happened, Emily was disappointed. I felt I was fighting a battle for Veronica, because she was not here to fight it for herself. I got a lot of satisfaction from proving things to be untrue, with the result that eventually Emily stopped running things by me as she was slowly running out of material for her book.

One complete falsehood that was published in Emily's book was the tale that accused Veronica of stealing papers from the drawers in the Fianna Fáil rooms when she worked there, and leaking out information, which eventually appeared in a story in the *Phoenix* magazine. Emily asked the editor of *Phoenix*, who was probably one of Veronica's best friends, about this, and he assured her that Veronica was not the source of this story. So Emily asked a question which she knew he would not answer – to reveal his source – and this he refused to do. So Emily decided to go with her own theory. She ran this damaging rumour with no regard whatsoever for its consequences.

I remember one day Emily telling me about how inexperienced Veronica had been and that she had never checked her stories. Emily said she herself would never run a story without verifying the content. That day I thought that I would put that to the test, and decided that in one month's time I would contact Emily with a good story. Emily knew about my relationship with a particular family and I used this as bait. We had arranged to meet in the Hollybrook Hotel in north Dublin, where many a political scheme was plotted, and, during our chat, I slipped into conversation a totally untrue tale that the father of this family had been hit with a tax bill for IR£1.7 million. Emily probed and I reluctantly gave her the details of the settlement.

Emily ran the story, although of course she told me she had checked it with contacts who could confirm it. The following Sunday I read about the family's settlement on the front page of *The Sunday Business Post*. The details, which of course I had made up, were exactly as spun to Emily, including the precise figure I had quoted. This told me a lot about why Veronica was so successful. She would not have run the story without confirming it and, through her many contacts, would have soon established that it was rubbish.

In her book Emily recalled an occasion when I visited her home. In her account she claimed that, like Veronica, I 'knew what buttons to push' with reporters and that I always had an agenda.

She also claimed that I promised her interviews that I failed to deliver, but that she eventually got an interview with me 'in which I cried for the first time ever in all the times we had met'. I feel this is an extremely unfair account of what had happened between us. I accept I had an agenda; it was to protect Veronica from someone whom I knew had never liked her and in turn she had not liked back. The interviews, which Emily described in her book as half promised, then promised and then not delivered until one day I just arrived at her house, does not fit with her description that it was the first time I cried in all the times I met her. Also, I would never attend someone's home unless invited at a specific time. I certainly do not remember crying, but who knows, I may have been trying to push one of those buttons which, according to Emily, I knew to push.

I do recall delaying doing the actual taped interview until I had satisfied myself as to exactly where Emily was going with her book.

My call to Emily's home was a return visit. She had already visited my home yet she neglected to include an account of that particular evening in her book. My recollection of her visit to my home is as follows: like some of her colleagues who attacked and disliked Veronica, Emily tried to be charming, but unlike Veronica herself, she had no idea what buttons to press. During our conversations prior to this, I was always well aware that Emily had an agenda of her own and knew what this was, but never could get her to drop her guard and admit it. On this particular occasion Emily came to my home, brought wine, smiled, drank some wine, drank more wine, and, close on a year after we met, dropped her guard. When she outlined her plans regarding her book, I suspected that she intended to try and damage Veronica's memory. Emily eventually left in a taxi, and I smiled to myself thinking, 'Never drop your guard with the enemy.' There are some things I remembered from my Fianna Fáil days.

In the end, Emily broke every promise she had made to me. She failed to talk to my family, yet had promised she would. She failed to allow me to see a copy of the portion of the book which related to my interview with her, yet had promised she would. She failed to remove the swearing from my text, yet had promised she would.

In the months and years that followed Veronica's death, some of her colleagues caused immense suffering to our family. I will never be able to bring myself to forgive these people as they caused so much unnecessary hurt to my mother. During his time as editor of *Magill*, Vincent Browne commissioned a piece that, in my view, was no more than a character attack on Veronica and it showed no regard for her family, most importantly her son. It was Veronica's time at the *Tribune* that is the root of the problems she had with her colleagues.

Veronica came late to journalism and it is probably this more than anything else that caused the difficulties that she experienced with some of her colleagues. She was constantly on the front page, winning awards yet, in their eyes, still only a blow-in. This would have driven Veronica on. She knew how to succeed and got on with her work, and more importantly she ignored those who bitched because they were jealous. Veronica had careers that failed, but so what? She had the drive and ability that allowed her to pick herself up and move on. This is what separated her from others. If Veronica set herself a goal, she would achieve it. It was this same stubbornness, however, that was probably her downfall. When those who were the weekly target of her pen tried to intimidate her, she became more determined to expose them. The reality is that Veronica cared, and those colleagues who called her reckless just don't know what it is to be committed. One thing that is particularly sad is that if Veronica's colleagues had recognised such commitment in someone from another profession, they would have praised it in their writing. However, when the person succeeding is one of their own, they not only fail to recognise it, but they see it as reckless.

***

Soon the nation would be shaken by this awful crime and an investigation, unprecedented in the history of the state, would begin. It was an investigation that would see the most talented of the state's investigators working together under the leadership of the force's most respected policeman, Assistant Commissioner Tony Hickey. The success of their work was soon evident. Some 3,500 statements were taken, millions of pounds in cash seized and 75 people charged with crimes that were solved as a result of enquiries. Hickey was joined by some of the forces most elite members, including Superintendent Jerry O'Connell, Inspectors Todd O'Loughlin, John O'Mahony, and many other talented Gardaí who worked long hours in an attempt to solve this horrible crime. The criminal thugs were so arrogant they had no idea what lay ahead and thought that after a day or two the heat would die down. Hickey and his men had different ideas.

***

Let me repeat, nobody is untouchable. Nobody who orders a
crime in a democratic society can be allowed to be untouchable.
Then Taoiseach John Bruton speaking about Veronica's murder,
26 June, 1996

The reaction in the Dáil to Veronica's murder, combined with the public outcry, ensured that no effort would be spared in bringing those responsible to justice. The investigation had its headquarters in Lucan Garda station and Hickey gathered around him some of the finest investigators in the force. Once his team was in place there was an air of confidence that the perpetrators of this awful crime would be caught.

Veronica's murder was seen by many as an attack on society. The men who were involved had become so arrogant that they believed they were untouchable. They had at least one garda on their payroll, they had accumulated a huge arsenal of weapons and they had carried out many gangland killings over the previous twelve months, none of which were solved. The Gilligan drugs gang had established itself as one of the most feared and respected gangs in the world of organised crime.

Veronica's murder was a direct challenge to the state of law, a clear statement made by criminals, and for the sake of society it was vital that these amoral men be brought before the courts. Hickey had a mammoth task, but he also had the backing of the people, and more importantly he had unlimited resources available to him as he set about catching those who murdered Veronica.

The Gardaí were well aware of the impending assault case between Veronica and Gilligan. From the start, his gang were the number-one suspects, but there was little in the way of evidence to help the Gardaí construct the case against them. The case took a dramatic turn, however, when Charlie Bowden, decided he would turn state's evidence. This was the break the Gardaí needed and it came a lot sooner than anyone had expected.

***

Charles Bowden was arrested on 5 October, 1996. He was the second member of the Gilligan gang to be arrested; Russell Warren had been arrested the previous week on 30 September. Initially Bowden denied any knowledge of the murder, but slowly he told what he knew about the crime and the background to it. He claimed that he had decided to turn state's evidence after he was shown pictures of Veronica on a dissecting table, full of bullets. He said that he then felt shame and remorse. But Bowden is not the sort of man to be overcome by grief, indeed he would have been delighted that Veronica had been murdered and would have believed, like the other gang members, that with her out of the way it would be business as usual in their drug dealing business.

So why did Bowden turn against his fellow murderers, and what exactly was his role in her killing? Bowden is an extremely intelligent man. The reason he decided to turn on his partners in crime had nothing to do with remorse. He knew that the game was up. Soon the Gardaí would find the hundreds of thousands pounds that he had hidden at various places around the city and they would discover that he was the man who leased the building that was used as the distribution centre for the Gilligan drug business. Gardaí had already recovered some of Bowden's money from his brother's house. The net was closing in.

Bowden had other reasons to be fearful. During the course of interviews, he was aware that the Gardaí knew who the main gang members were. They knew that he was the gang member in charge of weapons; he was the man who always got the guns ready when someone was to be shot, and they knew that his involvement in Veronica's murder went even further. I believe Bowden decided to turn state's evidence in an effort to save himself, and it worked. He agreed to give evidence in the trials against any of the gang members who came before the courts, and in return was provided with a written undertaking that he would not be prosecuted for the murder of Veronica. For Bowden it was win, win, win. For the Gardaí it was a huge risk, one which Assistant Commissioner Tony Hickey was brave enough to take.

There is no doubt that Bowden was overpaid for his co-operation. When he appeared before Judge Cyrill Kelly and pleaded guilty to drug and gun charges, we watched as this self-confessed murderer, who admitted to cleaning and loading the gun which was used to murder Veronica, got a light sentence. I knew the size of the risk that was being taken. It was hard to see him be treated lightly by the courts, and when Veronica's former colleagues started to bet on the sentence he might receive, I found that distasteful. In the end, Bowden received a six-year sentence for drug trafficking.

The remaining cases now depended on the credibility of Bowden's evidence and his truthfulness to the courts. This was a big mistake. It transpired that Bowden could not provide sufficient evidence to allow a case to be brought against the man he claims actually shot Veronica. Furthermore, he did not have the evidence to uphold the murder charges against Gilligan in court. Bowden's evidence in the case against Paul Ward, a trusted gang member, was so dishonest that Ward had his conviction for Veronica's murder overturned on appeal. We paid a large price for Charles Bowden's evidence, but this man who got immunity, received a light sentence and who is being looked after in luxury by the state, has turned out to be useless to the state. The murder gang are using his lack of credibility and reputation as a liar to help secure their release.

All of the judges that Paul Ward appeared before came to the same conclusions about Bowden. In the judgement delivered in the People v Paul Ward on 27 November, 1998, the President of the Special Criminal Court Mr Justice Barr said, 'The court accepts without any doubt that Charles Bowden is a self-serving, deeply avaricious and potentially vicious criminal. On his own admission he is a liar, and the court readily accepts that he would lie without hesitation and regardless of the consequences for others if he perceived it to be in his own interest to do so.'

In the same judgement Justice Barr added, 'The court is satisfied that the reason for his conversion to the alleged truth had nothing to do with remorse as he contends, but is the product of a cold dispassionate assessment of his grievous situation at that time and amounted to a decision on his part to extricate himself as best he could from what he probably perceived to be the reality of his situation then.'

These judgements are so accurate that one questions why the police allowed the success of the whole Lucan investigation to rest with Bowden.

However, with Bowden on side, the investigation moved along at an unbelievable pace. In October 1996, Paul Ward was arrested and was brought before the Dublin District Court and charged with conspiracy to murder. This charge was later changed to murder.

***

Paul Ward, the first to actually be charged with Veronica's murder, was the thug who made the remark, 'This one is for you, Veronica. Who says crime doesn't pay?' on a video made at a Meehan family wedding in St Lucia in March 1996. That video was of vital importance to the investigation as it clearly established who Gilligan trusted. It showed that Paul Ward was one of Gilligan's most trusted and closest lieutenants.

Paul Ward, originally from Crumlin, had purchased a house in Walkinstown from the proceeds of his drug business. He was a common criminal with many previous convictions who fitted perfectly into Gilligan's gang. He was also a drug addict who was in a serious relationship with Vanessa Meehan, the sister of Brian Meehan, second-in-command of the Gilligan gang.

On 18 October, 1996, Ward was brought before a night sitting of Dublin's Bridewell Court and charged with conspiracy to murder Veronica. Ward's trial took a long time to come to court and it would be two years before he was eventually convicted of Veronica's murder. On the evening of 18 October, I was at home watching the news. It was the first I heard about Ward being brought before the courts. The gallery was full of reporters, onlookers and those who had an interest in the proceedings. However, none of Veronica's family were present. I felt that this was wrong and that someone should have been there for Veronica as she would have been for anyone she loved. That night, as I watched events unfold on TV, I pledged that I would attend, when possible, all of the trials and hearings relating to Veronica's murder. This was a decision that was easier to make than carry out, but with the help of Louann, I rarely missed any of the hearings or cases over the next four years.

Following Ward's appearance at the Dublin District Court on 18 October he was remanded to appear in Kilmainham District Court at 10.30 am the following Thursday, so Louann and I headed off for our first day in court. We were taken aback by the large media presence and the public interest in events, but soon learned that this would be normal at Veronica's hearings.

The first day we arrived at the court most of the seats were already taken. We noticed some empty seats in the middle of the second row and excused ourselves as we made our way to them. We soon realised that we had just seated ourselves smack in the middle of the entire Ward family. There on either side of us were the siblings of the first man to appear in court charged in relation to Veronica's murder. We decided not to move and sat it out, staring straight ahead while this drug dealer, who played his part in murdering my sister was brought into the court. Naturally, he turned to his family and started to wave. We just sat there, and I took satisfaction in knowing that this was the beginning of a process that would see Ward and the others in his gang locked up for the rest of their lives.

On one of the days in Kilmainham District Court, I noticed a lot of activity among Ward's sisters at the back of the court. I watched and wondered what was going on. Suddenly, as Ward was to be led to the dock, he turned around and started to talk to a young child. She was waving frantically as her aunts pointed her to her daddy, who said, 'I'll get ye something for yer birthday later, right.' Ward had just had his first contact with his daughter since his arrest.

The appearances at Kilmainham were difficult as most of Ward's family stared at us and tried to intimidate us as we entered and sat in the court. Kilmainham also proved to be a learning experience. In future we made sure that we familiarised ourselves with the family and friends of the accused.

On one occasion when I attended the court as depositions were being taken, I was alone in court with Ward's family. We sat and faced each other as we waited for the court officers and legal teams to come back to court following the lunch break. As we were waiting, one of Ward sisters, who seemed to lead the rest of his sisters, asked me across the court, 'What are you fucking looking at?' I smiled back and ignored her questions. Her brother Paddy Ward told her shut up. I laughed to myself, as she could not hide her hate for me. It was obvious that they were finding the truth being revealed about their brother difficult to accept.

Paddy Ward was always courteous and mannerly, even though he was convicted for bribing the corrupt garda, John O'Neill, who was on the payroll of the Gilligan gang and who signed passports for members of that gang when they were fleeing the country after the murder. Paddy Ward used O'Neill to look after driving summonses for a member of his staff, but had no dealings with O'Neill in relation to any of Gilligan's business. In court on the day of Paddy Ward's sentencing in 1998, Inspector Todd O'Loughlin, the number two in the Veronica murder hunt, described Paddy Ward as a 'law abiding, hardworking individual with no previous convictions'.

It was never easy for Louann or me to attend these hearings, but it seemed no problem to the Ward family. They showed neither shame nor remorse. They seemed to accept that their brother was no more than a drug-pushing thug.

Attending court each day brought new revelations. The hearings started each day at 10 am and finished at 1 pm when they broke for lunch before the afternoon session which ran from 2 to 4 pm. These were long trials and they were taking over our lives. It was important to attend, but one also had to continue to make a living. There were still children to be dropped to school and homework to be done. Louann and I had made a decision that we could not allow the various cases to disrupt our children's lives. It meant that I would be in work in the mornings at 7 am to do a few hours work before court commenced. Then, in the evenings, I would catch up on the shortfall. Sometimes I would get home at 7 pm; sometimes it would be many hours later. It was harder for Louann. She could only attend court in the mornings. She would have to leave court, sometimes after hearing extremely upsetting testimony, and go straight to pick up our youngest child. The children would be aware from media reports and from us that the trials were ongoing, but we would never expose them to the details.

We got to know each of the gardaí who worked on the case and grew to respect them as the trials went on. For the first few weeks we had to park in the ILAC Centre and walk to the courts. During the first trial, it was not just members of the Ward family who attended court, but the family members of others in the gang as well. At times they would stare at us as we went to and from court, and in their own stupid way try to intimidate us.

On one occasion we felt that we may have been followed, and after mentioning it to Assistant Commissioner Hickey, Louann, to her embarrassment, was provided with an escort of two plain-clothes detectives as she walked to her car. A solution was then found which saved valuable Garda time and Louann further embarrassment. We were authorised to park alongside Garda cars at the front of the court. This made matters considerably easier for us.

The evidence of Ward's involvement in Veronica's murder is very clear. At 8.15 am on the morning that Veronica was shot by the Gilligan gang, Ward received a call from Brian Meehan, the man who drove the bike on which the gunman was passenger. At 8.30 am Meehan phoned again, and again at 8.40. The two men were regularly on the phone to one other. At this time, Ward was monitoring Garda radios. Planning was to precision and the gang had to succeed or Gilligan had a problem. What never came out in court is that had these thugs failed, Gilligan would have had others look after it for him. He needed Veronica murdered and he would have it done.

Gilligan believed that money could buy whatever he wanted, including the life of a young mother who was causing him problems by proceeding with a case of assault against him. Had it been necessary, Gilligan would have broken up his gang of thugs. Ward and the other gang members were making thousands of pounds each week as Gilligan's distributors. Gilligan had let it be known that there were many others who could run errands for him and who would be glad to murder Veronica, and they could take over his distribution business. Everyone knew where they stood. Gilligan was not the only one who would lose out if he went to jail. So the gang members were taking no chances.

Ward called Meehan at 8.50 am and again 9 am. He called from his mobile, even though he was at home. Having satisfied themselves that communications were in order, the men went about their tasks.

At 11.02 am Meehan called Ward on his mobile phone and six minutes later the call was returned. Mobile contact was in order, no chances were taken and the evil plan commenced. At every stage of this operation, Ward was kept fully informed of what was happening. The gang members who were to shoot Veronica had been told that she was on her way back from Naas. They had received their call. At 12.49 pm, just six minutes before Veronica was shot, again they called Ward. The call lasted three seconds. No doubt he was being advised that Veronica's murder was about to happen. At 1.06 pm, Ward received another call from Meehan and this call lasted almost 37 seconds. Long enough for Meehan to boast about the killing and say he was on his way. Minutes later, it was alleged in court, they pulled into Ward's back lane and then washed themselves before heading into town to start work on their alibis.

The motorbike was eventually recovered in the Liffey River, but the gun has never been found. Had the bike and gun been disposed of in the same manner, one would have expected to find them both together.

Ward remained busy and phone contact was maintained between Ward and Meehan throughout the day. Ward was keeping the rest of the gang advised of Garda movements. His last call was at 11.11 pm, when he spoke with Meehan for nearly five minutes. Ward was not with the rest of the gang later that night as they celebrated Veronica's murder in the Hole in the Wall pub and then back at Charlie Bowden's house.

The conviction of Ward was a victory for the Gardaí because they had started to smash the gang. However, if this case were to be judged in isolation, then it could rightfully be called a disaster. Some of the most experienced investigators in the state were slated by the trial judges who accepted the word of Bowden, a self-confessed murderer and liar, rather than the word of respected officers. The court also said that there was some element of doubt about alleged verbal admissions noted by Gardaí during Paul Ward's interviews, and wondered if in fact these had been made at all.

There were many long and difficult days in the Ward trial, many judgements to be given, and often the trial was held up as the legal teams made their way to the High Court or Supreme Court in an effort to have a decision that went against them overturned. At one stage there was talk that the prosecution would withdraw the charges rather than disclose to the defence certain witness statements that were made. These statements would not have helped the defence anyway, but at one stage it looked like the case would stop because of them. The Supreme Court came up with a compromise, the judges in the Special Criminal Court would view the statements and satisfy themselves that withholding them was not damaging to Ward's defence. Difficult as it would have been, I would have agreed fully with the decision to drop the charges rather than show the statements. These were given in confidence. They included statements from prostitutes that worked for Gilligan, girls who knew damaging evidence and were brave enough to come forward with it. There would be no justification in releasing this information to the gang and endangering these girls.

I remember sitting in court and awaiting judgement in this matter, thinking how Veronica would feel if this case were dropped. I was then prepared for whatever the outcome; I knew that she would say, 'Don't tell them, drop the case.' She would have said time would win out against the likes of these and how right she would have been.

The Ward trial produced many trials within trials. I was often annoyed that respected police officers were being questioned about their tactics. There was a lot made about the fact that the Gardaí had brought in Ward's girlfriend, Vanessa Meehan, and his mother for questioning. These people were well aware that Ward was a criminal and was involved in serious crime. You don't make IR£275,000 a year from petty crime. The investigating officers were trying to pressurise Ward to speak. They wanted to know what he knew about the murder, as they had evidence that he was involved. They were not only depending on the word of a supergrass who may have been lying to protect himself, there was other evidence as well such as the phone calls. There were also other witnesses coming on board. The police were involved in the biggest manhunt in the history of the state, and they had in custody a person they believed played his part in this brutal killing.

I found it hard to watch the smirks on the faces of these thugs being tried for murder as the team from Lucan were cross examined as to their *modus operandi*. I think they were right to arrest Ward's mother and I think they were right to arrest his girlfriend. If experience had led Gardaí to believe that by bringing them in it would exert further pressure on Ward, well good for them for doing so. These men were trying to establish Ward's involvement. They believed he knew where the gun was and they wanted to locate it. A number of officers were criticised in the Ward judgement, criticism that was, in my view, extremely unfair.

The court found the following in its judgement handed down on 27 November, 1998: 'The court is satisfied beyond all reasonable doubt that the visit from Mrs Ward [Paul Ward's mother] was a deliberate ploy, devised and orchestrated by the police in a final effort to prevail on the accused what he had done with the gun ... The court is satisfied that the visit was not arranged for any humanitarian purpose, but was a cynical ploy which was hoped might break down the accused and cause him to make what was perceived to be a crucial admission regarding what had happened to the weapon ... In all the circumstances, the court is satisfied that in the interest of justice and fairness all admissions allegedly made by the accused during his period of detention at Lucan Garda Station must be ruled inadmissible.' It is this type of criticism that makes it harder for those affected by terrible crimes to come to terms with a tragedy.

Despite the criticism levelled at the investigating Gardaí's handling of the case, in November 1998 Paul Ward was convicted of murdering Veronica. When the judgement was delivered, Ward's legal team expressed confidence that he would succeed when he appealed. They were right. On appeal, Ward had his convictions overturned.

On 22 March, 2002, the president of the Court Of Criminal Appeal, Mr Justice Francis D Murphy delivered a 20-page judgement where the court set aside the conviction and sentence of Paul Ward. They found that the evidence of Charlie Bowden was totally unreliable. They also said that other evidence in his original trial indicated that he could not have been part of the plans to murder Veronica because he was due to be in jail the day the murder was committed. A warrant had been issued and Ward was to serve a month in jail for driving offences, the only reason he was not in prison that day was because the Gardaí had not called to arrest him. The defence's contention was that Ward would hardly have been included in such an elaborate plan if he were due to be in prison on the day the murder was to be carried out. Other evidence given by Bowden, which placed Ward at locations where he could not have been, were taken into account, and it was the view of the court that Bowden was trying too hard to implicate Ward in this crime.

Ward is now serving a sentence for his part in the Mountjoy riots where five prison officers were held hostage and threatened with blood-filled syringes. Had he not participated in these riots, he would now be a free man and walking our streets.

***

The first trial where we saw supergrass and self-confessed murderer Charlie Bowden perform in the witness box was in the trial of drug dealer Patrick 'Dutchy' Holland. Through clever questions and answers, it was made apparent in court that the Gardaí and investigating team at Lucan believed Dutchy Holland had shot Veronica.

Of all those who stood trial for Veronica's murder, Dutchy Holland seemed to be the most distant member of the gang. He was a loner and a typical psycho. His trial began on 18 November, 1997, and sitting alongside him in court each day, it was easy to believe that he could kill a person. This was not the first time I had come face to face with Holland. He was a printer, having learned his trade in Arbour Hill Prison and on one occasion he had used the services of my print company. Holland served his time with Malcolm McArthur, the killer of Nurse Bridie Gargan. Holland also knew a lot of people in the printing trade, who I have spoken with, and they all agree that he was a dangerous criminal.

On one occasion when Holland had purchased a machine from a reputable dealer, the machine gave teething problems. The normal procedure is that an engineer would be called out to rectify any problems. Holland had a different way of dealing with it. He went with heavies to the home of the supplier to insist that his money be returned. The supplier was also warned not to report the incident as there would be serious repercussions if he did.

Holland was the first of the Gilligan gang to face trial, although he faced no charges relating to the murder of Veronica. This was a pity, as I would like to have heard his story. I have made contact with a number of people that act for Holland and they insist he had no part to play in her shooting. I have also spoken to Holland and others known to him and each tell the same story. Their question is why he would have returned from the UK if he had been the shooter? The fact is that Holland was not charged and no evidence was ever produced to indicate that he was responsible for the shooting other than the untruthful testimony of Charles Bowden.

If we have only the word of Bowden, then I must say that I cannot judge Holland on just that. I have raised my doubts about Holland's role with many gardaí, journalists and indeed criminals over the years. None have been able to provide evidence that Holland was the gunman. On one occasion I raised my concerns with a senior officer who was central to the investigation. I asked him what evidence other than Bowden's testimony there was to suggest that Holland had shot Veronica. His reply was that Holland was in Dublin on the day of the killing.

Gardaí let it be known that they believed Holland was the pillion passenger who shot Veronica. In court during his trial, the arresting garda said that he was detained because she had information that led her to believe that he had shot Veronica. I raised questions about what evidence was available to link Holland with the shooting with a few gardaí and some journalists when I was doing an interview at TV3. Within days of my questioning Holland's involvement, I was approached by a well-known crime reporter who tried to convince me that Holland had shot Veronica. He said that the reason he knew this was because senior gardaí had told him. He insisted that not only had Bowden named Holland as the gunman, but there was also other evidence, which I would learn in time. Now, over eight years after the murder, this other evidence is still unknown to me. I attended most days of all of the trials, and from the detailed cross-examination of Bowden that I witnessed on many occasions, I still remain unconvinced that Holland in fact pulled the trigger.

There is no doubt that Holland would be capable of carrying out such a cowardly and obscene act. This, however, does not mean that he did. Holland returned to Dublin and was convinced that he would only face charges in respect to drug dealing. Although he tried to sneak into Ireland using a disguise, he was not fearful of facing the drug charges and was confident that he would win his case. The only hard evidence linking Holland to the drugs was a list found at the gang's lock up. This list contained the names of those who were supplied drugs by the Gilligan gang. This, combined with the testimony of Bowden and others, along with Holland's unexplained wealth, was enough to secure his conviction. This also linked the person the Gardaí believe to be the busiest assassin in town to the gang and also Veronica's murder.

Holland was born in 1940. This alone separates him from the profile of Gilligan's gang, the rest of them being younger. He served his first sentence in 1965 when he was found guilty of receiving stolen goods. He was again convicted in 1981 for the more serious crime of armed robbery and was jailed for eight years. Later he was found in possession of gelignite in his flat in North Strand, the arresting officer on that occasion was Tony Hickey.

Holland was different in many other ways to the rest of the gang. He was devoted to his wife and mother. He came from a good family which had no previous involvement in crime, and he was not part of the set that spent their drug money in a *nouveau riche* manner in nightclubs and going on holidays to the Caribbean Islands and other exotic locations.

Holland was 57 when he was convicted of drug dealing with Gilligan's gang and will be in his late sixties before he is released. Although he was sentenced to 20 years for the importation of cannabis, this sentence was subsequently reduced to 12 years on appeal. He was sentenced in 1998 and, with remission, will be due for release in 2006. Holland seems to have no problem doing his time, unlike the other Gilligan gang members serving in Portlaoise. According to one prison officer who guards him, he is a model prisoner.

During Holland's trial, when Bowden was cross-examined by Senior Counsel Patrick McEntee, I began to have my doubts about Holland's involvement. The more evidence that was introduced trial after trial, along with Bowden's demeanour and his inconsistencies, resulted in my believing that it was Bowden who had carried out the actual shooting. Bowden, who was an army sniper and former champion marksman, had admitted to having handled the gun and having loaded the bullets that killed Veronica. He could not properly account for his movements on the day Veronica was shot.

***

Garda John O'Neill was a crooked cop who had fallen on hard times because he overspent in his everyday life. He was in huge debt and most of his wages were deducted from his monthly cheque to pay back Credit Union loans. He had many other borrowings, which he was unable to pay. O'Neill gave in to a weakness of greed, and sold out to a gang of thugs who were playing Mafia and believed they could buy anyone or anything.

O'Neill was as bad if not worse than the scum for which he worked. In a twelve-month period he received IR£16,000 from Gilligan's gang. They now owned a policeman. The gang used him for many things, although we will never know the full extent of his dealings with them. O'Neill had travelled full circle in just five years. In 1990 he received the Scott Medal for bravery when he tackled an armed robber who confronted him. Yet, just five years later, he was assisting the gang responsible for a horrific murder, signing false passport forms so that those same murderers could flee the country.

When he was arrested by Detective Jerry O'Connell of the Lucan team, O'Neill admitted his involvement with the Gilligan gang and went to Lucan Garda station. Here he confronted Paul Ward and told him that he had admitted to looking after summonses and signing false passport applications for Gilligan gang members. O'Neill regularly met gang members and fed them information on the investigation into Veronica's murder. On 3 April, 1997, former garda, John O'Neill, was sentenced to four and a half years for corruption.

As his colleagues tried to pursue this gang, O'Neill was keeping them up to speed with the investigation and trying to help them evade justice. The evening he was arrested, I received a call from Assistant Commissioner Tony Hickey and Inspector Martin Callinan, who had been working with my family. They asked to meet me and told me about O'Neill. I knew this was hard for them and I respected their forthright approach. They knew there would be bad press and that this corruption would reflect badly on the force. As far as I was concerned, however, this gave me reassurance that the cream of the force was involved in this investigation, and whoever involved themselves with this gang would be brought before the courts. I knew then that no effort would ever be spared to find Veronica's killers.

***

Bit by bit, Gilligan's evil gang was falling. The number two in the gang and the man who drove the gunman on the day of the killing, Brian Meehan, was arrested along with his partner in crime, John Traynor, in Holland on 10 October, 1997. Meehan had fled to Holland and was moving around Europe in an effort to avoid arrest. It was believed that the two men would face serious charges and that the extradition of both would be sought. However, this was not to be the case, and one of the big unanswered questions in this whole saga is why Traynor was allowed to walk out of custody.

Many believe that Traynor was an informer and was protected by senior members of the force. Others suggest that, when he was running his brothels in Dublin, he filmed many people in compromising situations and these people were now protecting him.

The extradition of Meehan was a long drawn-out process, but he was eventually returned to Ireland on 3 September, 1998. So, after a year in custody and over two years after he murdered Veronica, Meehan was about to face justice.

Meehan's first appearance in court after his extradition was brief. It took about 20 minutes for the charge of murder and other drug-related charges to be put to him. He also applied for free legal aid. Things were now falling apart for the untouchables. Ward's trial was due to begin in less than a month and now the number two in the gang was locked up with his friend. During Meehan's trial, tapes were played in which he threatened the life of Charlie Bowden's wife. This was damning testimony and played a big part in showing the court that this animal would think nothing of killing a person.

The evidence of state witness Russell Warren was accepted by the court, and it was found that Meehan had in fact driven the bike which was used to transport the man who shot Veronica. It was also at Meehan's trial that his Senior Counsel, Terence McCrudden, suggested that it was Bowden who had shot Veronica. It all ended for this hard man on 29 July, 1999, when Meehan was found guilty of Veronica's murder and was sentenced to life in prison. It was a nervous judgement and it took nearly an hour before I realised that Meehan was being found guilty. So the man who thought he had it all would no longer swagger about in his designer clothes that he bought from his IR£275,000-a-year drug dealing. There was a great sense of satisfaction as this thug was led away to spend the rest of his life in prison. It was, we all hoped, the beginning of the end.

***

On 6 October, 1996, the same day the Gardaí discovered the drug distribution centre at Greenmount, John Gilligan was stopped as he attempted to board a plane to Amsterdam at Heathrow Airport with £330,000 in his briefcase. The arrest of John Gilligan was a cause for celebrations for those of us who loved Veronica. When he was detained in the UK, I realised it would only be a matter of time before he was brought back to Ireland, but still, I attended a number of hearings in Belmarsh in southeast London.

I always remember the first time I set eyes on this man. I had flown to the UK that morning and when I arrived at the court I was extremely tense. I remember approaching the court and photographers from some Irish papers running ahead of me, taking shots. For some reason unknown to myself, I lost it and became abusive towards them, yet they were only doing their job. As I walked into the court I returned to them, apologised for my behaviour, and walked the road again so they could get their picture.

I went to the public gallery for Gilligan's court appearance. I was alone as the press and gardaí from the Lucan investigation, including Assistant Commissioner Hickey, were in the body of the court. When Gilligan was brought into the court I could not believe my eyes. He was such a small little man and yet he had caused so much destruction.

As soon as I saw Gilligan, I remembered the video of the Meehan wedding in March 1996, where he and his inner circle had celebrated on the Caribbean Island of St Lucia. I thought to myself that it would be a long time before this bastard would enjoy the sun again and play the godfather at another wedding in St Lucia. The video had proved helpful in establishing that Meehan and Ward were all well known to Gilligan, who had tried to deny that he was the leader of their gang. I always remembered the image of Paul Ward saying to the camera, 'This one is for you, Veronica. Who says crime doesn't pay?' He thought he was so smart. The video also showed that Veronica's assault case against Gilligan was something that was on their minds even so many thousands of miles away from Ireland. It proved that not only was it a problem for Gilligan, but the rest of his gang was aware of his pending difficulties. That event was just three months before this gang murdered Veronica.

That first day I saw Gilligan at Belmarsh Court was 8 September, 1997. It was obvious that Gilligan would try every tactic to delay his inevitable return, but in the end he lost his battle and was extradited back to Ireland on 3 February, 2000. The long battle to have Gilligan returned to this jurisdiction was won. Since his detention in October 1996, Gilligan had had the best lawyers and tried every angle to prevent his return to Ireland. Now he knew that he would face justice. I honestly believed that we would see him convicted for Veronica's murder, but regrettably this was not to be. However, when he landed in the military plane and was arrested in his yellow prison suit, it sent a clear message to all criminals – no matter how much wealth a man has or how much he is feared, the rule of law wins out in a democracy. This was a great day for all of us. Not only for Veronica's family, but also for the investigating gardaí who worked so hard to bring this evil man to justice.

I had seen Gilligan many times in court before he arrived back in Ireland, and had become used to facing him and being close to him. I rushed back to Ireland when the decision was handed down to send him back, so I could attend when he was brought before the Special Criminal Court. I went straight to Green Street Courthouse and met Louann. When we went to the court, we sat and waited patiently for him to be brought in and charged. Louann and I were alone, and I felt a great sense of victory that Gilligan was to stand in an Irish court to answer charges of murdering Veronica.

When we left court that evening and were driving home, I noticed that Louann was crying. I asked her what was upsetting her, and she replied that it was seeing this monster in person. Louann had sat through many difficult days in various court hearings, but none had upset her like this day. It was the fact that Gilligan had beaten Veronica up, ripped her clothing and violated her as a woman that upset Louann so much, and now Louann had to sit a few feet from this man.

Gilligan, who had last been sentenced for a crime in 1990, and who had pledged never to return to prison again, was on his way to Portlaoise prison. This made me feel good, and even though we all knew he would try to frustrate the justice system, no one in Green Street was concerned about the eventual outcome. Gilligan originally said he would defend himself, then appointed lawyers and dismissed them, but eventually his trial got under way on 4 December, 2000.

It was a long and difficult trial. Throughout, Gilligan tried to intimidate Louann and me, often acknowledging us in the morning. This bastard, who was complicit in the execution of my sister, would make smart, cocky remarks like 'Hi Jimmy'. I sat through this, confident that he would be convicted for Veronica's murder; little did I know that I would be proved so wrong.

Thursday, 15 March, 2001, was a day I will never forget. I had awoken and prepared for our day in court. This day would be different. This was judgement day in the Gilligan trial. We had waited nearly five years for this moment, and even though I was tense, I never doubted that Gilligan would be convicted of Veronica's murder. This was the only charge that concerned me. I was not interested in the other charges against Gilligan; the one that mattered was murder. We sat there for hours with the men from the Lucan team, who had given endless hours and made personal sacrifices to bring this man to justice, as the judgement was read out to the court. As it turned out, this was the first time that a case would fall because of Bowden and Warrens' testimony.

As the judgement was read it became apparent that there were difficulties, and I began to feel physically sick as I realised that Gilligan would be found not guilty on the charge of murder. I remember turning to a detective who had worked on the investigation from day one and telling him I was going to be sick, his words of comfort were all that prevented me from making a scene in the court that day.

I asked myself how a court could say: 'While this court has grave suspicions that John Gilligan was complicit in the murder of Veronica Guerin, the court has not been persuaded beyond all reasonable doubt by the evidence which has been adduced by the prosecution that that is so and, therefore, the court is required by law to acquit the accused on that charge.'

I was not the only one shocked at this decision; the entire courtroom had believed that Gilligan would go down. There was disbelief amongst the Lucan team that they had failed to secure the right verdict.

When the judges returned after lunch, Gilligan was sentenced to 28 years in prison for his role as leader of what was the biggest drug-dealing gang in the history of the state. He had only been found guilty on the charges relating to the supply and distribution of cannabis. Many took comfort from the fact that he received a long sentence, but I knew that we had lost, in reality we had been denied justice.

As Gilligan was heading to serve his sentence, Bowden was preparing for his release. Now the man who cleaned the bullets and loaded the gun, and who could not account for his movements at the time of the killing was about to be rewarded for giving evidence in court that the trial judges had found so unbelievable. The Garda Commissioner questioned how judges who had accepted the evidence of Bowden and Warren in earlier trials could not do so now. In my view, the answer to that is simple, the more they appeared in court and were cross-examined by counsel, the more obvious it became that they could not be trusted.

The reality then began to sink in. It could only be a matter of time before the convictions that had been secured on the evidence of these unreliable supergrasses would be overturned in upcoming appeals. Bowden flew off into the sunset with the hundreds of thousands of euro that he had made from his drug-dealing activities, money that had not been seized by the Criminal Assets Bureau, along with whatever payments he had received from the state, yet only one man would be convicted of Veronica's murder.

***

The perception of Veronica's legacy tends to be firmly rooted in the formation of the Criminal Assets Bureau and the new level of awareness that exists about the drug problem in Ireland. Sadly, the drug situation is worse now than it was back in 1996, and as such reporting on this subject today has become repetitive and boring.

However, the largest part of Veronica's legacy remains unaddressed. She was much more than a journalist. She was a sister, a daughter and a wife. More importantly she was a mother to her son Cathal from whom she was so cruelly snatched on the day of her murder. Cathal and his devoted father, Graham, who was a loving husband to Veronica, are left with only photographs, second-hand stories and a few years of precious memories to remember her by.

***

There was worldwide interest in Veronica's story, with articles appearing all across Europe and America and television documentaries being made by the BBC and NBC. Hollywood had also shown an interest as early as 1997. It began with an article by renowned journalist Mike Sager in American magazine *GQ*. The piece was entitled 'The Martyrdom of Veronica Guerin'. It was this moving and well-researched piece, combined with other smaller pieces she had already read, that convinced Disney Executive Vice President Susan Lynne that Disney's Touchstone Pictures should produce a film about the 'Gutsy Guerin'. At this time, Hollywood's number-one producer Jerry Bruckheimer became involved. He and Disney decided to acquire the rights to Sager's article.

These were not the first big Hollywood names to express an interest in making a film about the life of Veronica. There had already been talks between the rest of my family and Steven Spielberg, these however had come to nothing. Susan Lynne despatched a number of researchers to Dublin and they began looking into the story. They contacted Veronica's husband, Graham, and my mother, and were told that a firm of solicitors were acting for the family. Talks took place, but terms could not be agreed. This did not deter Hollywood, if they want to make a film they will and if the family co-operates, that's fine, but if not, they go ahead anyway. For years the Kennedy family in America tried to stop films being made about them and failed, so the Guerin family didn't have much chance in stopping the Hollywood machine.

It was only when researchers returned to America that I learned from a film correspondent that they had been here. I then contacted Susan Lynne and told her that I had just heard of their visit and I would like to speak with the person who was writing the script. Lynne was surprised, she had understood that no family members wished to co-operate with the production. I told her that I felt it was important that a family member should speak to their staff. I was acutely aware that there were many critics in the media who were queuing up to give their spin on Veronica.

Lynne was delighted, but insisted that this could not be done over the phone, so three days later, scriptwriter Carol Doyle arrived back in Dublin. Over the next few days Louann and I spent many, many hours giving Doyle our insight into Veronica. We watched family videos, looked back on old pictures, and went drinking with old boyfriends and friends of Veronica's. We did what we could to show her the type of person that Veronica was as we wanted her to hear it first hand from people who had known Veronica all her life. When Carol Doyle went back to America, in her own words, she understood what made Veronica tick. I was glad that we were able to influence her opinions and help her to form a more accurate picture of what Veronica was really like.

We heard no more for many months and believed that this, like the hundreds of other projects that Disney start, was now shelved. This was not to be the case, however, with one man making the difference. Jerry Bruckheimer had become determined to see this project through, it was passion, not business. Why would a man who makes $500m movies be so determined to produce a film with a budget of $30m? The reason is he had real admiration for Veronica and wanted to tell her story to the world.

Disney had now passed all their research over to Bruckheimer productions and it was they who proceeded from that point.

Although they still had no director, they continued to work on the script. It was late 2000 when the script was completed, and when executive producer Chad Omen sent me a copy I was delighted with it, and knew that we were right to have assisted. Joel Schumacher then came on board as director as he liked the story, and as he himself had suffered as a result of drug barons. Joel had been a drug user when he lived on the streets as a teenager, so he more than most knew the battle Veronica faced as she tried to tackle Gilligan and his gang. He set about working with Bruckheimer and together they sought out a leading lady.

It seems that luck was on the side of this project when Cate Blanchett agreed to play Veronica. There was now a formidable team in place and the project looked like it was unstoppable. After many discussions with Chad Oman, I received a call asking if I could make myself available for a week to go through the script and story, and talk to the team about Veronica. They also wished to see places of importance: her home, her workplace, and where she had grown up.

Joel and Cate arrived in Dublin on Sunday, 9 September, 2001, and I met with them and their assistants on the Monday morning. As soon as I met them I knew that both were passionate about this project. They were also extremely sensitive about Veronica. At this stage I was the only family member who approved and at the outset had explained that we would not be able to call to my mother's house or meet other family members. Forever the professional, Joel said that he fully understood and was confident that, in time, they would accept the project. While this did not happen when the team visited Ireland on the first occasion, my mother did come on board about half way through the shooting, which would have been early April 2002. This meant everything to Joel and he was now more confident than ever that the movie would be a success.

Joel was the ultimate professional, he studied everything in great detail and during their first week in Dublin the team visited many of the locations that were to play major parts in the film. They travelled the journey from Naas Courthouse along the Naas Road. They met with former sources, met friends of Veronica's and studied the court case reports to familiarise themselves with the cases and evidence as it unfolded. They sought a meeting with Assistant Commissioner Tony Hickey, who kindly gave his time to assist in what, at this stage, we could only hope would be a fitting tribute to Veronica.

As the week went on we could all feel that it was going to be a great movie, any concerns that we had about aspects of the script would only have to be pointed out and the views were taken on board. Cate was pregnant and filming was planned around her availability. A place to live was sought for and her family, she looked at a number of locations, and eventually found a suitable apartment on the southside of Dublin.

Cate is a perfectionist in everything she does, just like Veronica was. I sent her many hours of footage, tapes from Veronica's TV appearances, home videos and I know she spent many hours just studying Veronica's habits. She and Louann went off one day and talked about the type of clothes that Veronica wore and the fact that she always wore earrings, Cate sought the smallest detail as she prepared to act the role of Veronica. She spent time in the offices and just watched how it worked, talked to her colleagues, spending many hours with them, always learning, always listening. In reality Cate and Veronica were so alike, both professionals and both determined to do a job well.

However, it was constantly at the back of my mind that Hollywood makes movies for entertainment, and sometimes they have to create and embellish things to make a film succeed. This was always a fear and even though I felt confident, I still had niggling doubts. However, saying goodbye to Joel I told him that whatever way it turned out, I knew he cared and wanted to produce a tribute to Veronica. There is no doubt that this is what he did and all who loved and cared about Veronica will forever be indebted to

Joel Schumacher and Jerry Bruckheimer for producing what was a wonderful film.

On Sunday, 3 March, 2002, filming began. Louann and I visited the set on the first day along with our sons, and we brought a gift for Cate to wish her well. We met with her husband, and seeing her at work with her new baby, Dashiell, with her husband beside her, she seemed perfect for the part. Like Veronica, her work was important, but to have her family around her meant much more. Cate was relaxed and was looking forward to the challenge of the part, and I was confident that she would play her role well. When I returned home from the set, a courier had been to my home and had delivered a letter that Cate had written that morning.

'It seems that making this film is finally a reality, my family and I are here, and today is the first shooting day. I am still trawling through the reams of information on Veronica in an attempt to unfold her courage and determination, her humour and her humanity. Her life, personal and professional, was so rich and full and her spirit so deep and complex it seems an injustice that we have a mere two hours to capture her essence, to tell a tiny fragment of her "story". I wish I had the privilege of having known her. I know I cannot hope to become Veronica, a life force such as she only graces the planet once, and inevitably, her character will be filtered through me, but to the best of my ability, I passionately wish to understand her and the world in which she operated.'

Reading Cate's letter and having got to know the people involved in the production of the film, I knew we could look forward to a tribute to Veronica being produced. The film was more than we could have asked for. When it appeared at cinemas around the country I felt really proud, proud to have had such a wonderful sister and proud to have played a part in what will be a lasting tribute to a wonderful person.

***

On 3 November, 2004, two more members of the Gilligan gang were arrested in Amsterdam. Peter Mitchell and Shay Ward, a brother of Paul Ward, were found in possession of ten kilos of cocaine and two kilos of heroin. The arrests were the result of a joint operation between British and Dutch police forces. No attempts will be made to extradite the two men until they have completed any sentence they may receive in the Dutch courts.

***

The investigation into Veronica's murder is all but over, and while some of the main players are in prison, only one has been convicted of murder. Two who admitted to murdering Veronica are enjoying a new life at the taxpayers' expense. Each year will bring more appeals and soon some members of this evil gang could be back on the streets.

In 1996, I said of Veronica:

'I don't look on her as a heroine. Bring her back tomorrow and put another thousand kilos of cannabis back on the streets and I would really have to say, I couldn't give a shit about the drugs; I'd rather have my sister back.'

My views have not changed since then, and hopefully they never will.